LONG LENS:
NEW & SELECTED POEMS

LONG LENS:
NEW & SELECTED POEMS

Peter Makuck

AMERICAN POETS CONTINUUM SERIES, NO. 121

BOA Editions, Ltd. ❧ *Rochester, NY* ❧ *2010*

First Edition
10 11 12   7 6 5 4 3 2 1

For information about permission to reuse any material from this book please contact
The Permissions Company at www.permissionscompany.com or e-mail permdude@
eclipse.net.

Publications by BOA Editions, Ltd. – a not-for-profit corporation under section 501
(c) (3) of the United States Internal Revenue Code – are made possible with funds
from a variety of sources, including public funds from the New York State Council
on the Arts, a state agency; the Literature Program of the National Endowment for
the Arts; the County of Monroe, NY; the Lannan Foundation for support of the
Lannan Translations Selection Series; the Sonia Raiziss Giop Charitable Foundation;
the Mary S. Mulligan Charitable Trust; the Rochester Area Community Foundation;
the Arts & Cultural Council for Greater Rochester; the Steeple-Jack Fund; the Ames-
Amzalak Memorial Trust in memory of Henry Ames, Semon Amzalak and Dan
Amzalak; and contributions from many individuals nationwide.

See Colophon on page 182 for special individual acknowledgements.

Cover Design: Sandy Knight
Cover Art: "In the Distance" by Sherryl Janosko
Interior Design and Composition: Bill Jones
Manufacturing: BookMobile
BOA Logo: Mirko

Library of Congress Cataloging-in-Publication Data

Makuck, Peter, 1940-
  Long lens : new and selected poems / Peter Makuck. -- 1st ed.
     p. cm. -- (American poets continuum series ; no. 121)
  ISBN 978-1-934414-32-3 (alk. paper)
  I. Title.

PS3563.A396L66 2010
811'.54--dc22

                                            2009029836

BOA Editions, Ltd.
Thom Ward, Editor/Production
Peter Conners, Editor/Marketing
Melissa Hall, Development Director/Office Manager
Bernadette Catalana, BOA Board Chair
A. Poulin, Jr., Founder (1938-1996)
250 North Goodman Street, Suite 306
Rochester, NY 14607
www.boaeditions.org

NATIONAL
ENDOWMENT
FOR THE ARTS

NYSCA

for Phyllis

Contents

New Poems

from Off-Season in the Promised Land *(2005)*

from Against Distance *(1997)*

from The Sunken Lightship *(1990)*

from Where We Live *(1982)*

New Poems

Long Lens

I

After she gave me her camera
for my weekly trek through three counties
and asked for photos of anything
she might improve into a painting,

those flatlands rose to attention again—
tobacco barns, most of them tumbled
or slumped, some smothered with kudzu,

or those three men with shotguns,
orange vests drifting through corn stubble
behind tracking golden retrievers,

or that barrel of flames by a shack
where two black boys warmed their hands,
then dribbled, shot for a rim nailed to a tree.

But poverty is an easy score
and not what had me parking
next to a barbed wire fence by a field
drifted along its furrows with a snow

of cotton the harvesters had left.
On the field's far side, a house
of white clapboard with a tin roof.
In the yard, on blocks, a black Chevy,

(like the one I had as a teen), but what
held me wasn't some proud idea of prevailing—
it was a roofed-over well with a bucket,
and between two pines a wash line

waving its dazzling sheets, blue jeans dancing,
red and yellow shirts bloated with wind.
Fenced out by sharp wire, but focusing
a long lens over the distance of a winter field,

I saw my mother, a tan wicker basket
at her feet, reaching down clothes.

II

Folding laundry, I can see our clothesline
waving its patches of color like the flag

of a foreign country where I had happily lived
in a small clapboard house surrounded by pines.

I can hear my mother in her strong accent
saying she didn't want a dryer

even when we could finally afford one—
Our sheets won't smell of trees and sunlight anymore.

An art book I bought in Paris
tells how poor painters like Van Gogh

and Gauguin bought the cheapest pigments—
colors that destabilized faster than they knew.

Folding and sorting, I look out a window
that frames whitecaps chalking the chill-blue bay.

Hell, all colors fade—anyone does laundry
knows this, Dad and I joking, then talking

about a cheapskate judge we worked for once,
but his money helped to pack my suitcase

with new clothes and put me on a train
that took me to a college four states away.

III

For a week of blowtorch days in July,
we had graded and paved a winding driveway
for this Quaker Hill judge. He watched us

from his high study window
and from the cool hum of his gabled house
emerged only once—to underpay us at the end

because the job took three hours less
than our guesstimate. I had shoveled and raked,
pounded stakes for the 1" x 6" wooden borders,

wheel-barrowed load after spilling load
from the cement truck chute. Then together
we sawed the screed, long and heavy, back

and forth in a thirsty slanting light.
That red evening, hotter and later than usual,
sweaty, our clothes full of dust, my father

and I bounced down our lane in his truck.
At the last rise our house lurched into view
and he stopped. What was he looking at?

Wash was waving in the back yard, just behind
our well with its pulley and bucket. His face
seemed painted by something lost,

then he smiled, and we jounced ahead
toward my mother, lamb chops, roasted potatoes
and the good cool water from our well.

Gray Fox

All morning I've watched the snow fly,
looking up from a page of the same color.
Sometimes wind will rattle the shutters,
creak the joists and rafters
as if the house were talking to itself.

My window frames a white emptiness
until suddenly, as if conjured, he's there
maybe twenty feet from the glass
with a limp rabbit, long hind legs
dangling from his jaws.

At home here
before our house was built,
this gray has apparently decided to stay.
Though at a holiday fish fry,
our wined-up neighbor mumbled
about abnormal behavior,
rabies, 12-gauge buckshot the cure.

Last week, luckily downwind,
on a path that edges the salt marsh,
I watched him inch through eelgrass
then leap high
into a twisting dive on a vole—footage
I've been playing since,
but wanting to see him again
and here he is, looking like a Wyeth,
drawn to answer some need.

He stares right at me
but does he know what I am?
A man either bored
or afraid of the empty white hours

that make me grateful
for shape and color,
something animate to attach to—
a sharp wise face,
ears cocked and aimed, rusty flanks,
and a black-tipped tail
that triggers much more than delight.

Release

With rod and tackle box,
I'm slogging through soft sand,

a red sun going down in the surf,
swag-belly clouds drifting in

with Ray, only two months dead,
going on about girls that summer

we studied French in Québec and
guzzled Labatts at the *Chien d'Or,*

about how he'll marry again, keep
at it until he gets it right—*Pas vrai?*

Above the tide wrack, a woman
in a two-piece with half my years

kneels struggling in the sand
with a pillow of feathers,

one wing flapping—a pelican
tangled in fish line, treble hook

in the bill pouch, the other in its wing.
Ray says, *Ask her out for a drink*

but she says, *Could you give me a hand?*
I drop the tackle and secure the wing

while she croons to calm him and
with one free hand untangles the line.

With pliers from the tackle box,
I expose the barbs and carefully clip,

a total of six loud snaps. Then I hold
the bird while she frees the last tangle

and we step back, join the onlookers,
a father explaining care to his kids.

The pelican now tests his wings, rowing
in place. He looks around and seems

to enjoy the attention, just as Ray did
in bars, buying drinks and telling jokes.

But this college boy with a can of Bud
is no joke and says they watched it flap

all afternoon from that deck on the dune.
His buddy agrees with a belch

that buys a round of frat boy laughter.
Ray tells me the kid needs his clock cleaned

just when the pelican waddles up
and puts his soft webbed foot on mine.

He tilts his head to catch my look, then
flapping runs into the air, tucks his feet,

and climbs, turning over our small circle,
before heading west. Dazzled and dumb,

I'm faintly aware of the woman, then gone,
weightless and soaring over water, looking

down on myself slogging through sand,
certain that I'm being watched,

if only by another self
who will have to tell how it happened.

Deo Gratias

Behind a skirt of hydrangeas
was a crawlspace door that led to a crypt
where the bones and skulls of old pastors
lay scattered about,
    or so we believed,
until candlelight for the first time wavered
and vault covers lay in a row.

The eighth grade altar boys made us do it.
Like sneaking wine before Mass,
or munching down a host or two,
    but this ritual was after novena
when Mr. Marino, the old sexton,
locked up the church.

As if on a mission,
we'd emerge from the crypt
into the basement hall
where Boy's Brigade marched us
in tight formation on Friday nights
    toward this about face,
this passing through the kitchen
up spiral stairs
to the vestry, sacristy,
then down the main aisle—
the nave quiet with outside wind,
the ghosts of black widows
whispering Aves in loud Italian—
past the holy water stoup,
    up to the choir loft,
twisty bell tower stairs,
and the chortle of pigeons.

Once, slightly drunk, in my mid-twenties,
something brought me back,
     then as now,
for one final climb above the black
habits of nuns, the slaps,
the catechistic drills and Latin responses.
I saw that the wooden locker for my cassock
and surplice was no longer there,
but everything else exactly the same.
     I watched myself
step up to the parapet,
staggered under a skymap of stars,
blessed by the sight
of that hometown seaport glittering
like the jewel box of a bishop
flung open at my feet.

Caught

The book said *Argiope aurantia*
but it wasn't this Latin music
that caught and wouldn't let go.

That came later. It was the silk
filaments reflecting a low sun
at just the right angle, tiny beads

of dew on each strand, the whole
stretched between porch post
and roof beam. Then her—

black and bright yellow, body
about an inch long. Four lines
of scribbled z's converged

upon this "writer"
(according to the book)
perfectly composed, motionless

and ready. Her patience
puts me to shame. Each strand
is a word, artfully connected,

and I watch them waver
back and forth in a breeze,
regular as breath.

A perfectionist, she nightly
gathers and eats the web,
weaves and rehangs anew.

Her eight legs are black, but
red near the body
with that bright yellow glow.

I stand there looking
as closely as I can
until I have her, or she has me.

Ladybug

You forget the world
can quickly blur and wobble

at the chance landing, say,
of a ladybug on the wrist,

its orange the same
as your old Volkswagen bug,

the boot and back seat
filled with boxes and what

your father helped carry:
books, a green shaded lamp,

bookends, striped pillows,
blue blankets and sheets,

the hangered shirts and pants
your mother pressed last night,

a new suitcase and three
light bulbs ("Just in case")

he cushioned with wads
of the hometown paper,

your mother on the porch,
her sandwiches on the front seat,

her face shiny and red,
then turned to his chest

as you ease from the drive
toward a college four states away—

things buried for decades
until the ladybug landed,

on a blazing August afternoon.

A Closing Season

I've lapped this pool for twenty years,
hundreds of miles,
raced my son who easily beats me now
but swims after work by himself
in the far Pacific.

Sunlight on hex tiles trembles
in three places along the bottom of my lane.
I follow the black bar
down the middle, flip, spring off the wall
into the fading brightness of my own bubbles.

Twenty laps, then roll on my back
for a breather, for the clouds
that, lit from within, drift over the glass roof.
Ten more laps and I'm toweling off,
the pool still empty, soon to be drained,
the guard returning my card,
saying I'll need another
for the new rec center that opens next week.

He's reading *A History of Philosophy*
and as soon as I turn, he dives back in.
I watch the ripples subside, clouds
gone from the skylights,
following some path with enviable ease.

After a shower, I take my time, a last look.
A student my son's age clangs the locker doors
until he finds the right one.
I slip on pants and a shirt.
The scent of chlorine clings
with a feeling that won't go away—

not until the kid in the next row whistles
a melody I half remember,
and fumbling to fill out the tune, I hum
my way through a maze of dusty corridors
out into a colder sun.

Stopping

In the short shadows of noon, I'm driving
two-lane blacktop between long wide fields,
Getz blowing his way through a ballad,

heat shimmering up, warping the tree crowns,
turkey buzzards scattering from a white-tail carcass
in my hunter past, Getz perfecting nostalgia

until WORK AHEAD slowly grows into view
and I ease up to a guy in orange, leaning
on a stop-sign pole, walkie-talkie in hand.

The road runs past a guard in tree shade,
a twelve-gauge riding his hip, men
in state-issue orange, faces shiny with sweat,

dirt flying from shovels into the bucket
of a payloader by the ditch where they stand.
The red STOP looms and the kid talks

to his hand-held. He nods as if I'm telling
how years ago we hotwired an Impala,
cranked it up to a hundred ten on the pike,

ditched it, and never got caught. I'm still staring
at "Inmate" on his vest, when he turns the pole
from Stop to Slow. Moving again, I'm feeling

real heat for the first time. He grins and
gives me a thumbs-up sign, and I do the same,
passing the shovelers, the last guard with a gun.

Running

Practice over, the field and track are empty.
Nighthawks swerve after insects.
They screak, make dark unpredictable lines.
One dives close, its wings pant, joints creak.

These forty years later, our coach is still yelling,
telling me to get out the lead. On the south side,
by the creek, I hit a cold stretch with every lap,
like the chill I'd sometimes get on my Harley
of a late summer night in a back-road swale.

Sprint down that last stretch, then walk
in fading light with a good coat of sweat.
Clouds stretch like layers of fat.
A rabbit zigzags through the fresh mow, his
white scut disappearing under fence wire.

I jog through years of routes to the beach
at Fortune's Rocks around the university gym
to France and up the hill on the rue de l'Eglise
to the high school track behind my parents' house.

A panic of drying grass has me heading
toward home again. I huff up the steep hill.
The track lies below me—
that grave green mouth, those hard black lips.

Back Again

Up the hill past our old house,
across from the main gate
of St. Joe's Cemetery
    was always a flower shop
owned by the Dereloos
but the last time I stopped
in my rented car at sunset and

absently shuffled inside,
it had turned into a pizza joint—
no bright potted mums this time.
    Embarrassed,
I couldn't walk out,
    so I bought a small pie
and a beer to go.

Near the statue of the carpenter,
a worker of wood like my father,
I stood in the sinking light
and chewed the meatless kind
we always ate on Friday.

I sipped the Bud my father liked,
made small pieces
of the crust and scattered them
on the plot, a beige stubble,
that was far too narrow
to contain him.

The stillness was loud,
the graveyard deserted, birds settling
in the nearby woods
but thronging

to the feeder he made
for the window of our TV room
where he laughed with my mother
at sitcoms and the antics
of birds and squirrels that
tomorrow, a Friday morning,
would breakfast on pizza above them.

Pilgrims

Merchants, scholars, priests,
recent soldiers, and liberated wives,
we travel from different states in a six-hour jet
to stroll at our ease
in the April after-rain sun. In a group
of nine and twenty, we move with our guide, small,
under the chiseled saints
of Florentine and Roman masters,
unshaped by the vision
that moved their hands and rested on absolute law.

But we want to feel
and do it by climbing
(with a 100 lire ticket) Buonarroti's dome:
up the damp, narrow stairs
that twist through floors, trees, and tile red roofs.
Around the dizzy ramp we look down
on saints who had just looked down on us
and furtively hunt for a clean spot
to scratch a durable name.

Descending slowly,
we think of sunlight and Italian trysts,
the stubs in our pockets like permission to forget.

Cité Bleue

The resort is not quite finished—
Algerians still work on the grounds.

Palms and the blue-green Med
remind us of the Florida Keys.

We watch their dark faces
behind shovels and barrows. Or they

watch us on the sly
walk through the olive grove down the beach.

It's a condo we've borrowed, the distant
Cap d'Antibes like a painting in our window.

One Pernod and the twilight's walking with ghosts:
Fitzgerald, Hemingway, MacLeish.

Where were the immigrant
workers when tender was the night,

the parties endless and
living well was the best revenge?

There's more wine in the kitchen
and in the back window

cooking fires flicker.
Shadows leap at a packing crate shelter.

Two workers play at a last game of *boules*.
In the corner of the casement

as if in a Breughel, a man
in a burnoose pisses on a tree.

Artful shadows in a fiery dark.
A cold night wind gets up,

and I return to the table,
the wreckage of dinner,

and pour more wine,
but the mistral has begun to moan.

Toledo, Spain

What has stayed in mind isn't
so much the blue Islamic designs,

or reflecting pools in the Alcazar,
or the Santa Cruz with so many

paintings of stylized Annunciations,
Nativities, and Assumptions

but this guy pulling suitcases,
three large wheeled bags, one

attached to another, a train really,
clack clacking in front of the café

until they get stuck on the curb.
Face glazed with sweat, he loudly

clears his throat as if to speak
but aims instead an angry look

at his young, tight-skirted lover
lagging behind at a boutique window,

a look that says
the least you could do is help

this miserable bag-train over the curb,
which she does, watching me

watch her bend beautifully,
then blesses me with a wink and a smile.

Last Run at La Plagne

The skiers pause,
postpone delight, pick steep
trails that plunge away on both sides
of a crest, sharp
as a knife.

The opposite peak
is where the avalanche was—
that slow-moving wave over three bodies
that migrate into May
unseen as fishes.

The hood of Mt. Blanc
in the distance. Shadows
stretch. I could drop to Champagny.
Or back to friends
at La Plagne.

Once only.
A warm scent of woodsmoke
floats up from the valley, up with a yodel
like a gift from a dark
tangle of trees.

I imagine myself
in the finals of the giant slalom,
a long tracking shot, tucked, spraying
powder—a run remembered
in some book.

I could end
against a tree, a carom
of flying skis, my body endlessly bouncing,
the camera following my lone ski
to a merciless halt.

But I know
Swissair will fly me out.
I'll quickly lose my snowtan. Pale,
I'll ghost about the office
unseen as anyone.

Magdalene at the Mirror

After Georges de La Tour

Scholars tell us he beat up a peasant
caught on his land,
was brought to court and paid a fine.
How could such a man
have painted such a saintly face?

But that man didn't, another did,
one more hidden,
and I'd like to think he had to,
had to pay with pigment to a watchful dark,
and more than once.
This other always looks out from a dark mirror,
measuring, appraising,
regretting the one seen daily
in a proud round of the village streets.

Once, when the power failed, my father
lit a hurricane lamp
and placed it on the kitchen table.
Ending a long silence, he wrote to his father.
I listened to the nib scratch paper
and watched his face in the wavering light.
I'd never seen him so absorbed,
his face so deep
he was another man that night.

Magdalene sits in the same reddish light,
her fingers at the eye pits of a darkened skull.
Forget who she is.
A face from another painting could serve as well,
a cutpurse or a cardsharp
or, in an off-white kerchief, a gypsy girl—

that lovely oval face looking innocently askance
while her hands clip the mark's gold chain.

She's who she is, but someone
more familiar too, like my father,
hauled into a court of truthful light,
or me, or you watching midnight
compressed to one small room,
a tincture lethal to the candle bloom,
hand on bone, purity at last,
the mind returned from its vain solo trek
to a mirrored face of full of shadows,
knowing at last the one truly duped.

Behind Shackleford Banks

Hunkered against the wind
with a live-bait rig on the bottom
and not another boat in sight, I'm anxious
for a spring that won't arrive,
some kind of break in the leaden light,
binoculars at the ready
for wild ponies that refuse to appear
over the tops of dunes
and down along the white stretches of sand
when that gray scud gets close to lethal
and has me on the verge
of fishing for the dearly departed.

Instead I get hooked on a storm petrel
I'd only seen at the Gulf Stream, fifty miles out,
never inshore of the island,
not fluttering as usual like a lost butterfly,
but hovering at first,
feet pattering over watertop lightly
with a slip and a slap of Gene Kelly magic,
then wings fixed
casting for new angles
on the hard east wind,
going for the ground effect cushion
to soar,
only a foot off the surface,
        pitch and yaw
to a rhythm deep inside—
a deific sight
that extends and lifts everything
to a new level of light.

Awake

Above the winter channel, a bright moon,
clouds on the move, a tug
pushing a barge, its nav lights plowing south

down the sound's far side, maybe a deckhand
in a bunk below the wheelhouse
reading a book that could alter his course.

I duck inside, shivering from our top deck
and climb into a bed
that is already warm with her sleeping.

My book light brightens the print,
a Russian peasant by a campfire where I left him
on the steppes under stars,

dreaming of tomorrow and the wedding,
good vodka, caviar, and dance.

Laughing Gulls

The moon sank in rough seas, a slick
of weak stars, a cold wind from the west,
tall waves tipping into a white seethe.

I'm drawn to this stretch of March sand
where a huge spotlight a half mile away
is pointed seaward from a motel roof.

Hundreds of gulls flicker like confetti
in the beam, cries rip the dark,
white wings plunge into thick schools—

a picture of chaos. But I'm not out here
for solace, just the habit of early
air along this hard unflattering edge.

Every year the tides churn away sand,
swallow boats and swimmers, or send
a bull shark into the shallows for blood.

The wind keens and flattens the sea oats
then suddenly drops to a whisper,
as if to mock my mood, tease me away

from some simple last line. At the motel
when I reach it, the gulls, all of them,
have settled on the surface, a rich lull,

a brilliant spackling of white on black
and a scent of bacon frying that floats out
and sweetens what darkness remains.

Flounder Gigging

Along the channel edges,
flats and shoals, even
with an underwater light you find
them hard to see.

They must pretend they're sandy bottom
with a concentration so complete
they disappear
into what they become.

Spinners

I had wanted to stay inside. Monarchs
had migrated. Cicadas littered the walkway.
Green-tail shrimp had fled to deep water.

It was time to haul the boat, winterize,
let it hibernate. Though sunny, a cold wind
from the north made the sound waves white.

Still, we loaded our gear and headed out.
A mile off the beach, leeward of the island,
out of the wind, we took off our jackets,

used planers to take our lures down deep.
As usual we followed arrowing terns
and crash-diving pelicans to the schools.

Right off boated a blue, and later lost
a heavy fighter twenty feet from the transom,
an albacore, that left me sadly unhooked.

Toward afternoon's end, our fishbox held
enough dinner for a dozen. That's when
splashes appeared to the south, geysers.

Then leaping bodies catching the sun.
I throttled back and eased ahead. Dolphin,
we thought, but up close they were sharks,

spinner sharks, rocketing up through
a huge pod of menhaden. Fin tips black,
undersides white, backs a blaze of bronze

as if from tanning all summer long.
Spectacular leaps, eight feet at least, rotating
two or three times in midair. Never

had I gotten this close. No telling
how long we stood in the cockpit watching
and wordless. All around us they were,

then suddenly gone. Nothing but the soft
slap of water against the hull, rising
and falling into deep swells. The sunset

had maybe ten minutes to go, the inlet
dangerous in the dark. Dave, never one
to profess, made a sweep with his arm:

This is the church that really matters.
Not a preacher can beat it. I remembered
it was Sunday, remembered I had wanted

to stay inside, in favor of what? Another
afternoon of back-to-back ball games?
I remembered finally to get us on plane

toward the inlet, where we turned west
onto a silver path of unearthly glitter,
cold wind burning on my cheeks like shame.

Getting There

After two pricey tickets for speeding
on Highways 17 and 43,
their endless billboards screaming
like previews of a coronary,
I had to slow down.
I had to sprout some new veins
and arteries through Carteret,
Jones, and Pitt counties,
find roads and places
with names like Fox Meadow Forks,
Doc Loftin's, Pete's Reach,
Buzzard's Corner, Pine Grove Chapel,
and I did too,
often seeing deer,
a black bear once,
and yesterday,
over a field of February milo,
a northern harrier
plunge behind a tobacco barn
with a wall that shouted: *Eternity
Is Just A Heartbeat Away.*
We're talking about getting to work
from Bogue Banks
all the way to Greenville
and on roads that make
the best of time.

Out of Aravaipa

From White Water Draw by the border,
after watching birds and still seeing the bright throb
of our first vermilion flycatcher through freezing rain,
    we headed north again. A distant checkpoint

on two-lane blacktop grew in the windshield.
Hand on his sidearm, a guard with shades
leaned in for our names and where were we from.
    A German shepherd with another guard

on a long leash sniffed and circled our Jeep
for the nothing we had to declare
but the glory of shrikes, eagles, and the high honking
    of a thousand cranes still floating in memory.

Rough roads climbed into Aravaipa Canyon.
We rattled over cattle guards past ashen scrub
and clusters of prickly pear toward The Chimneys
    that some old friends had told us to see

before a sign finally told us to stop—Flash Floods.
Road impassable, even for an off-road Jeep.
Lines of blue-black clouds piled up like curses kept
    to ourselves. The stillness didn't help.

After jouncing over miles of desert dirt roads,
we could only imagine those unearthly formations
sculpted by an outsized alien tripping on acid.
    So we turned about and headed for Bonito,

vowing to forget about goals, climbing switchbacks
out of Aravaipa into the mountains, around a curve
to a sudden vista—endless snow peaks, and
    long shadows taking the sage flats below.

Again we stepped into the unexpected, a glimpse
of a javelina disappearing into scrub, silence
now deep as the canyon at our shoetips. At first
    not a trace of the human in all this distance

then far below, like images from a lost language,
a mass of white, bonking and bleating, reshaping
itself before a herder on horseback and a border collie
    moving toward a corral in the quickening dark.

Trail

It turns along the canyon floor in low winter light,
down into and up the sides of a dried
river bed through palo verde and jumping cholla

that bumped against could set your legs on fire.
I lag behind, again out of tune
with too much talk, pretending to retie my boot,

and see him again, Paul, drunk and perched
on the porch rail, trying to tie
his shoe, teetering, then falling a good five feet

into a bed of blue and purple pansies where
he lay playing dead, arms folded,
Ray pouring beer, taunting, *Get up, you pansy!*

I kept seeing him laid out, but this time not
by laughter. He fell in the kitchen
and never got up, came word from his son.

This last of my college housemates laughed
long-distance a month ago, us trading
insults as usual, him saying he'd get there first.

What I should do is stop at the first bar I come to:
Joe, Ray, and me will be waiting.
We might even buy you a beer, you dumb Polack!

Here I stand looking down at Paul in the pansies,
resurrected in a way,
but still laid out, this desert air getting colder.

Darkness, like water, lifts from the canyon floor,
slowly climbs the redrock walls. My son
and his cousins are now far ahead, their laughing

voices faded into the repeated *cheets* of quail,
the shy song of wrens.
What am I doing? A few miles from the car,

off the trail, I pile some rocks into a small cairn,
mumble a prayer, and start to run,
watching for cholla, sweating and breathing hard.

A Lenten Observance

At the glass doors framing her deck, she stares at the birdbath—
a flowered platter from the kiln of a potter friend gone—

and hopes for something to see. She takes what the light
has to give, collecting details, trying to concentrate, to focus

through her own reflected image. She would turn the moment
into some modest kind of music beyond words. And it happens.

A red dot on the limb of a live oak fifty feet off grows in size
and lands on the rim of the platter, the same flaming color

she has seen in cathedrals, a prayer's echo just three feet away.
The cardinal sees her, and doesn't scare. Two deacon finches

and a white-throat arrive and take their turns in comic baptisms,
water spotting the glass as if shaken from a celebrant's sprinkler.

In The Daily Grind Café

Between yawns, I'm looking down
    at the white counter
      as if at a screen

that shows a cup of coffee,
    a silver spoon,
      and this leather

case that has ridden
    in my pockets for years.
      Now darkened in color

it has me suddenly viewing
    footage almost forgotten,
      Johnny saying, *Look,*

look at that blond . . . . You blind
    or what? Offering me
      his wire-rimmed specs,

the power just right
    to focus the blond
      who was sadly beautiful

because now I could see.
    How simple—just
      a smooth leather sleeve,

stitches on the bottom
    and side no longer white,
      cracked on the fold and

Dr. David Ginsberg
Optometrist
86 State Street
New London, Conn.

himself now gone with the gold
    print of his name
      but not out of focus.

In owlish glasses of his own,
    after eye charts and fitting,
      his crackly voice magnified

in this small room: *Peter,*
    you've been missing so much—
      Welcome back to the world.

from
Off-Season in the Promised Land
(2005)

Off-Season

All day the ocean's been burning
a cold blue that matches my mother's willowware,
the few cracked cups that I've kept.

I've come along a path through the dunes
to listen to the water's drunken repetitions—
that story about the *Wendy Lee,*
how she went down in rough weather last week,
four mothers made into widows.

Just off the bar, there's a shrimper hauling nets,
red and green running lights,
a Christmas tree in the oncoming dark.

A string of black scoters angles to the south, skims
a surface still lit with a last brandy tinge.

A scatter of sandpipers
works the beach in winter white, unbothered
by immensity, all dash and wistful peep.

I've wallowed in this windy emptiness before,
feeding a feeling that won't go away,
and won't become something else—a voice
you once loved, her hand on your cheek,
the way your father squinched his eyes when he laughed.

But reunion doesn't happen like this.
No lambent figures looming through cheap-effect mist
with a password that opens
the radiant purpose of all things.

What do I want? I know about the lost,
what search and rescue means—
every small thing is a clue. A single light comes on
in the long curve of off-season houses.

A pelican hangs overhead.

The shrimper is disappearing
but I still see a mate in dim light working the cull.
Gulls squall and flicker in the half dark.
Something invisible wants to be seen.

Dominion

Just off the blacktop
there's a silver marker,
black letters flaking:

*Union Forces
under General John G. Parke
landed here
on March 29, 1862
in the Fort Macon Campaign.*

In no time it hits you
that the "here" has moved,
retreated from a union
of greater forces—winds and tides
that sanded in the landing
and shoved the water
half a mile north,
the island in steady
advance on the mainland.

But the "here" now waits
for another defeat.
You can see for yourself,
become a rebel,
leave your car
in the Food Lion lot,
and hike down a sandy track

to Hoophole Creek,
a limbed-over tunnel
that at last opens
on the cordgrass flats,
wading birds, an adagio
of clouds, wide water, and sky.

But first take your time
in the grove of grandfather oaks,
those wide-spread limbs
dangling long mosses
of confederate gray.
It's thick shade, hard to see
at first the hot pink
fluttering from pounded stakes,
or belted around trunks
nailed in transit crosshairs
that will forever defeat

a place famous
to a few fishermen,
crabbers and birders
who can walk down a path
where flycatchers
and king birds dart
through the half light
and skirmish in an airy here.

General Parke took the fort.
Out of the north
a phalanx of dark clouds.
Hoophole flutters with deadly pink.
Only now is the same
and always that hunger
for dominion.

Empty Air

Twilight and snow are falling at the same time
whitening the empty street in front of our house

and the shortcut through Wilson's woods
that took me to the older boys on Clifton Street.

Our breaths looked like smoke
and lights came on in houses down the hill.

Mothers called from porches and
one by one our players left the game.

Now just Benny and Gary and me.
Gary spun the ball on his fingertip,

looked around, and said: *Practice time.*
Pete, go long and deep. On three.

Benny would hike. I knew the route.
Sprint down the right side to the culvert,

then zig to the middle where
Gary's great arm would have the football

spiraling down to my outstretched hands.
But, when I turned, the air was empty and

so was the street. Not even muffled laughter,
just snowflakes that are falling.

In the woods toward home, I stopped on the path.
Snow crystals ticked in the leaves. I stood

there for a time, not wanting a thing . . .

Truant

When the weather is right,
on the long drive to work, country roads all the way,
I stop at a bridge

on the Neuse River
and walk the span to loosen my legs and check
the riverscape changing.

Five minutes might pass
before a car does. Last week, an old farmer idled by
on a green John Deere.

His passing opened a huge quiet.
High water chuckled against wooden piers.
Mayflies glittered in the sun.

And the watertop was a black trance
until a light blue kayak floated into view below me—
a kid with a blaze of blond hair.

He leaned back, paddle
across gunnels, blades flashing, his face to the sky,
an appraiser on duty.

With me it was a lake,
an old canoe. I'd lie in the bottom, inspect the clouds
for shape, color, and size—my first job

to let the wind move me
toward some surprise, naming as I went: boot, nose,
horsetail—"Hey, are you okay?"

It was a county sheriff,
in a maroon cruiser, a white Stetson shading his face.
Did he think I was about to jump?

"You ain't got any ideas, right?"
I smiled and shook my head. *No ideas but in things,*
my smart-ass twin almost said.

But whatever ideas I had
had dissolved into a picture of that boy in the kayak
drifting with clouds.

"I was just looking," I said,
"Just looking," and stepped from the rail
toward one more hour at the wheel.

Spiritsails

They are out there again,
kids from the church camp,
beyond the jetty, their sails

old-fashioned white,
a small fleet of spooks
learning how to tack, luff

and find the wind
when none seems there.
Spiritsail,

just yesterday I learned,
was the kind with a spar
that tips ahead of the mast

on old coastal schooners,
and it comes back now
through these white sails

that turn black
when backlit
on this blinding plain.

Way off to the right,
all by itself, one boat stalls,
then starts back,

you talking about an aunt
who passed over, a cousin as well.
I fill in the blanks

with faces of my own,
that one sail rejoining the rest.
Faint cries and shouts,

a melody of laughter borne
by an onshore breeze.
They merge and eclipse,

part on opposite headings
before they tack and jib
as if in a dance

beyond the black jagged rocks
of the jetty.

Oceania Fishing Pier

We're jigging for blues,
sunset doing its fiery fade, showy
as the tourist couple that ambles out,
all spiffed in summer whites,
glasses of zinfandel, hot for something to see.

And as if to please,
a guy gets a screamer strike on a live bait rig.
Now a twenty pound cobia slaps the planks,
and the woman in white wrinkles her nose
with a line you might have predicted:

"He's not going to keep that poor thing, is he?"

Then it gets worse.
There's a trawler two hundred yards off the beach,
pulling nets through what's left of the sunpath,
a blizzard of gulls at the stern.

"So pretty," she says at my shoulder, "isn't it?"

No, it's *not* pretty, I want to say.
When you see a squall of gulls
behind a trawler on a sunset sea,
don't think beauty,
think bycatch: small blues and menhaden,
spots and croaker, unsellable mullet
littering the surface for acres,
feeding the gulls.
Think trawl doors that plow the bottom,
kill coral, fill the crannies
and hiding holes for next year's fry.
Think analogy:
harvesting corn with a bulldozer.

Pretty still echoes in the air,
and she *is* too.
Lips glistening with wine, she asks
if all this ain't pretty as postcard?

Looking down at the cobia opening
and closing its mouth, dying, slowly
dying, I tell her it is.

Wrasse

The ocean has a perfect memory
of who you are,
salt calling to salt, water to water,
and strips you
of family, job, and address
as quickly as you click the dive watch,
check the p.s.i., dump air
and ease down the anchor rope,
equalizing into the deep
blue world of waver and drift.

Three years and six stories down,
the *Indra* has started to ripen,
her steel gone orange with rust,
a long slow waving of kelp,
railings fuzzy but sharp
with urchins and barnacle rosettes,
quills that could inflate a finger
to twice its size.
Below decks, prison-striped spadefish
have made the passageway theirs,
the shower stalls too where hex
tile glows in your dive light.

A four foot barracuda by the bridge
circles more tightly
with that overbite smile,
darts and veers from your mask
at the last moment
to remind you how dreams need
to flex and test,
how angels   butterflies,
          blue hamlets and tangs
need crevice and crack,
how open water would turn them to snacks,

but not this wrasse,
yellow and no larger than a long finger.

A great grouper, amberjack, and sea bass
all wait in a loose congregation,
for his favors on the top deck
where clutches of tube worms
sway in the underwater wind,
opening and closing.

The way he bumps and frisks over each body
you'd think he was a narc.
The grouper keeps open its cave
of a mouth and he swims right in.
An impatient jack,
pectorals a-flicker, holds
for its turn by a bulkhead.
Under a frail peace, this yellow beauty
holds them apart and keeps them waiting
as he gets at tiny crustaceans,
lice, worms, and bits of dead skin,
slides into their gills
and into the face of every last one,
no matter how large or toothy.

You release the air in your vest,
settle on the deck like a buddha,
practice your breathing,
and watch the wrasse do its work,
each breath brightening colors
that could flower at the top
of this rising chain of bubbles.

Minding What's There

I'm browsing shell beds
and trying to work through
the one about who we are
when we forget to practice
who we are,

only half aware of the ocean
taking itself seriously,
a tall white tumble and hiss.
I should know the ebb
from flood by sound alone

but it's a clump of sea foam,
stranded and iridescent,
like an enlightened mind,
that tells me
about the effort of arrival.

Shells crackle underfoot,
bits of scallops and olives,
whelks and razors,
then a black isosceles
bigger than an arrowhead

stops my restless ramble
and has me stoop.
Two inches from base to tip,
shiny as obsidian, and sharp—
edges themselves tiny teeth,

a dark design, perfect
for ripping and sawing,
changed only in color
since fallen eons ago
from a jawful of others.

Its edge draws
a bead of blood on my arm,
those zigzag fins
beyond the surf zone at dusk,
sometimes an attack—

that girl we taunted
in high school ages ago
with "Sharkey,"
her sidelong glance
and crooked teeth.

I let it fall into the dark
of my pocket, testing
its edge with my thumb,
climb from the beach
and cross the road.

At the end of our drive
the neighbor's black cat meows
and sprawls for a scratch—
a sign of forgiveness,
perhaps even luck,

no junk in our mailbox to prove it,
pinetops giving sound to the wind,
the cat now rubbing my legs.
That sharp black tooth—
nothing I ever expected.

Hurricane Warning: Surfers

Around the bend slides an ocean eerie with storm light
and them at serious play: red and yellow wet suits, blue

and lime, their unconcern a reminder of something
long forgotten but now too strong to let go. Wind tugs

our pants and sleeves and has our hair fly back like spume
from the crests of fifteen footers rolling in. We lean

against the wind and hear the fringe of pampas grass
threshing above the beach where these boys worry

not a jot for tomorrow and make light of leaden swells—
a dream of Waimea Bay and the ache of endless summer

come at last to the Carolinas. Oblivious of snapping red flags,
riptides and undertows, they wait and wait for one moment

to lift them, a force evolving shape within us, making us
wait too, smile when the curl flexes and tilts them ahead

toward a lethal bottom of sand. How they tame the edge,
gravity giving way to a grace of their own making!

Some miss the moment and wait still, and when we leave
the island, exiled inland, I'm not even thinking of our house

turned to matchwood. Days later, through sweaty hours
of shingle and tack, chainsaw and tree limb, I still see

that boy farthest out, the one waiting past friends, now up
in one motion, wetsuit blazing orange, ready to defy all ruin.

Dusk Watch

We were sitting on the roof deck,
four friends with a bottle,
maybe six months after he died,

low sun melting on an emptiness
of ocean, waves almost quiet,
when into view floated a line

of brown pelicans,
hedge clippers with wings,
more than a dozen

in a slow motion glide
along a curving sickle of sand
suddenly veering,

wings motionless, fixed,
as if we were in somebody's sights,
Gerda saying they were his favorites—

characters comic
and soulful at the same time. Then,
as if called, one bird

left the cortège and returned,
turned tightly over the roof
four or five times,

the last an eye-level pass
before he angled off
to follow that long dark line.

We looked at each other
and finally laughed, Gerda too,
her eyes wide and wet.

We felt the wind
pick up, saw waves whiten,
but until the water went black

and the bottle was empty
we went on talking, nobody
saying a word.

In memoriam Bodo Nischan

Eventide

When you round Cove Point, the sun,
like a low red host, has migrated
west of the church steeple

over an anchorage of sloops and ketches
into what will soon be night
past the carcass

of a skiff almost hidden in the weeds.
You set down your bucket,
remove your sandals

and wade in with your net, just like the boy
last fall. He was happy
to show you

how to untangle the skirt, hold hemmed weights,
two gathers in your left hand,
the rest in your right.

Then you try tossing a full circle bloom
and discover that casting
a wide net isn't easy.

Hauling now, you feel a resistance, something
as needed as the ceremonial white scatter
of ibis farther out.

Menhaden and mullet wrinkle the surface
but shrimp stay hidden until a full net
gently thumps on retrieve.

Bead eyes, see-through bodies,
five black dots, four on the tail blades,
one for a heart.

Church bells ring against the rapt quiet.
Extra ecclesiam nulla salus sounds
from the past,

but the west is a great panel of stained glass
in this huge cathedral of air.

Prey

Coming from the pool
where I've just done laps, letting water bring me back,
I'm already elsewhere, thinking
about Tennyson and my two o'clock class
when a squirrel appears
ten feet from the concrete walk, by an oak.

Then a loud ruffle at my shoulder,
like an umbrella unfurled, before a flash glide
makes the Redtail seem to emerge from *me*

and nail the squirrel with a clatter of wings—
a long scream that strips varnish from my heart
                                before the sound goes limp.

She presides with mantling wings
over the last twitches of gray as I
edge closer to her golden eye.
She hackles her head feathers, tightens her talons,

holds me prey to what I see, watches me
as she lifts off, rowing hard for height, the squirrel
drooped in her clutch.

                        Now skimming a lake
of cartops in the south lot, making for the break
between Wendy's and Kinko's, she swerves up

sharply to land on the roofpeak of a frat house
over on Tenth.

Some noise from the world snaps me back.
I look about, but nobody has stopped
to look at me or where she stood by the tree,
only ten feet away. Slowly released,
I move ahead with the passing student crowd,
holding fast to what I have seen.

Into the Frame

You hike through a tunnel of live oak,
cool shade and wren song,

then climb the stairs that top out
on a high dune strewn with pennywort.

The sudden ocean and opening sky
make everything dizzy and unreal.

Like brightness after matinees
and those long treks home with friends.

But stop. Let this place erase everything
but itself, water a turquoise radiance,

sand a whiteness that stuns.
Just watch the young flood rushing

over ribs and welts, carving
new channels, mocking the known.

In the distance a red and yellow sail,
black patches on the water from clouds.

At your feet, a peach-colored canopy,
a man in a low chair lost in a book

and teens on a blanket lost in each other.
A father and son playing catch.

Middle distance, behind the bar, a boy
with blond hair and blue pail follows

a surge channel, an oxbow bending,
down the beach and out to open water.

He seems to be playing a secret game,
whispering, conjuring flow in the channel.

It's all like a painting, space between figures,
sun making sharp shadows, dramatic

clouds on the move, when into the picture,
in clear water, near the boy,

a dark mass like a shadow with silver glints,
an inky form that billows and compresses

but holds a shape—a school of finger mullet
trying to fool a longer lean shadow

that darts and swerves like the peregrine
you saw once stoop into a flock of starlings.

The boy sees it too, drops his blue pail,
and turns to call. Nobody is looking but you,

a hidden god who sees no need to intrude—
the fish a toothless cobia, not a shark,

now stuck in the oxbow unable to turn
at the low end, but the boy stoops,

as you want him to, and scoots it
over the shelf, then stands to watch

it clear and disappear
into deeper water with a lash of its tail.

No one, for once, shouted *Shark!*
Now the boy turns with what he has seen

to the father and brother playing catch,
the man in tent shade lost in his book.

The scene becomes a painting again.
Go ahead. Step into the frame,

descend one step at a time
to all that white sand, jade and windy light,

the boy still in you, latent but not lost,
running to tell you his tale.

Tight

Two of our table chairs
wobble when sat on,
she says,
or haven't I noticed
those wooden groans?
I turn them upside down
and see the years,
how they've loosened
high backs from seats
and mitered braces,
screws with no bite
in widened holes.
I'm looking at separation,
thinking
about thicker screws,
about switching to inch,
maybe inch and a half,
when my father
and his trick appear
out of a dark nowhere:
tooth picks or
a match stick
depending on the size
of the hole
that seems to grow larger
the closer I look,
an everyday small black hole.
I go with a match stick,
slide it in,
then the screw,
then turn to happy resistance,
the squeak of dry wood
the tighter I turn,
the black crack closing

to a mahogany seam
and we're tight again.
I wink at Phyllis, laugh,
and tap my Polack temple
just as my father did.

Roofers

Across the street, houses
are still black shapes, the ocean
turning amber in between,

then orange after coffee
and toast, red with the mayhem
of headlines that stop

at a first beating of hammers.
Three of them move around the roof,
around a Gatorade keg,

toting rolls of tar paper,
bent sideways with buckets of sealer.
A kid with long blond hair

shovels the shingles
that flap from the edge of the roof.
I bring him close with binoculars,

watch them rag the small guy—
Shorty from years ago,
whose answer was to grab his crotch.

Talk is the same—cars, women,
and getting high (an eye
out for the foreman's blue pickup),

the paycheck pool, a hot tip
on the fifth race at Lincoln—
the weekend just hours away.

The blond kid climbs to the peak.
He pulls off his shirt,
and hunkers down to a smoke.

A shrimper pulling nets
in a storm of gulls
keeps appearing between houses.

This room disappears.
Clouds drift seaward. Hands still black
from the tar kettle, no ambitions,

I watch what comes into view,
always eager for the small good thing
that happens next.

Another Art

The art of horseshit isn't hard to master.
People crave some color along the way.
Besides, how could it lead to a disaster?

Start small. Tell her your love will last forever.
At first it's not an easy thing to say
But horseshit's not really hard to master.

Soon, though, you should take the whole thing further.
How once you dined with Cher and Doris Day.
Amazing. See? This leads to no disaster.

Then tell about the time that as a golfer
You hustled Lee Trevino, made him pay.
The art of horseshit isn't hard to master.

That scar? From Nam, when hunkered as a sniper,
You caught a bullet for a friend one day,
But, hey, you're still alive—no great disaster.

Until before a judge and talking faster,
Now sworn to tell the truth, you're forced to say
The art of horseshit isn't hard to master,
Though it leads to (I lied!) complete disaster.

from
Against Distance
(1997)

Tangier Island

A mile above the Eastern Shore,
before we turn over water
in a friend's small plane, I see,
on the way to this speck in the Chesapeake,
the interlocking shapes
of green and plowed-brown fields
that put me in mind of Cézannes
I saw first in your class
at St. Francis on the coast of Maine.

Some wrote you off as "Silly George"
because you liked to laugh
with your whole big face,
but this is how you coaxed us
from ourselves to the enlargements
of philosophy and art—
the first for learning how to die, you said
(laughing, of course),
the second for learning how to see.

Climbing from the plane, I see
Maine for a moment—stacks of lobster traps
instead of crab shacks, pots and buoys.
I'm wandering
along these narrow lanes
more with you than my wife and friends.
You're explaining perspective again—

triangles and frames within frames,
light, color, and distance
around that waterman scraping his skiff
or family headstones
in a tiny front yard
where a woman rakes leaves
into a burning pile, the smoke

rising, then flattening in the heavy air
to hover like a huge pair of wings.

At the far end of the island, we turn
and face the distant houses
huddled together, barely above water.
One white steeple
tops the invisible triangle, fixes
the churning clouds and wind-bent trees
in this old Dutch seascape.

On my Renoir report
about "The Boatmen's Lunch,"
you wrote that *"joie de vivre*
is a gift,
and not a basis to evaluate painting."
I didn't know what you meant
until years later
when I saw you for the last time,
chemo-bald but undiminished,
smiling with your whole face,
radiant, like a bulb
before its filaments blow.

This island lives by the crab,
those red commercial emblems
a reminder of what you fought against,
what finally killed all color,
so I aim and focus
the water-doubled reeds of spartina,
still brown
but for a promise of green
at the base of each blade.
The shutter clicks
and a slide of Albrecht Dürer's
wild grasses are alive on our classroom wall.

As we bank toward home, I see
Tangier from the south at 5000 feet
looking like a medieval angel,
tilted forward, ready
to blaze through
a black wall of weather to the west.

In memoriam George Marcil O.F.M.

Dogwood Again

Home from college, I'd leave my reading,
climb the hill through trees behind the house,
listen to a rough wind suffer through
new leaves and, too aware of myself, ask why?

The answer could have been *stone wall,*
wind or some other word. In April, our house
lived in the light of those first white petals
and now I think more about hows than whys—

how, whenever we fished at Pond Meadow,
my father dug a small one up, carefully
wrapped the rootball in burlap, and trucked it
home until our yard blazed white all around,

and how, at Easter, those nighttime blossoms
seemed like hundreds of fluttering white wings.
Again that tree goes into the dark loaded
with envy, those leaves full of light not fading.

And this morning, a fogbright air presses
against the blank white pane and would have us
see the way mist burns from within, shimmers,
slowly parts, and flares upon an even whiter tree,

tinged now with orange, and how a soft fire
runs to the farthest cluster of cross-like petals,
each haloed with clear air, finely revealed.

Gray Removals

After a night of March winds,
I expect the yard to be blown away,
but my neighbor's out there grinning,
another squirrel in his boxtrap.
Twiggy nests that web the forks of limbs
have withheld the night. And squirrels,
either oblivious, or deliberately mocking,
chase each other, madly spiral his oaks (and mine)
leaping limb to limb, then over the roof,
along the powerline, and into another yard.

My neighbor is determined,
ready to transport his catch
deep into the oblivion of distant woods.
We're overrun, he says. The signs are everywhere.
Rain spilling from the upper gutter—
squirrels do that. They'll ransack your attic,
beat you out of your hard-earned pecans,
raid the seed in your feeder. Rats,
really just rats he's taking to meet
their country cousins. Same damned family.

As a kid, I used to shoot them
and nail their pelts to the barn door.
My trigger finger hasn't itched in ages,
but with my neighbor's right reason, I tend to agree,
yet early in the morning, when my body is heavy
and flexes like half-frozen meat,
I'd have them left alone, these gray ghosts,
let them land on my roof with a slap
and wake me with a rain-like patter in the eaves.

Three feet from my desk,
on the rain gutter,

like a jeweler with a gem to cut,
it rotates an acorn—crack, then feast.
Its eyes hold mine as it chews.
The air clears, as if someone had focused a lens,
removed a moment from the day
and made it lively forever.
Every time, I'll look up from my work,
take the bait, and be transported,
always confused when released, ready to run.

After

In the low afternoon light,
a row of cottonwoods led us out of Santa Cruz,
a small cemetery off in the desert.

That day, a few days before Christmas,
your father in front with me, I kept seeing your mom
not there in the back beside you,

and him, as I drove, stare through
the passing mesquite to some other place perhaps,
silence enforcing a distance.

Lame, he had held my arm,
looked down at the unhealed turf, then crossed himself,
thin shoulders quaking. I looked

beyond the wall, across
the creosote flats, and watched a coyote drag something
limp toward a culvert.

Back in the car, I kept seeing,
tethered to stones, all those mylar balloons—"Feliz Navidad"
or "Te quiero" in the shape of a heart—

emblems of another culture,
telling us how far from home we were, the balloons
tormented in the desert wind.

Before houses again rose up
and the lights of Phoenix hid a perfect indigo sky
where stars began to glimmer,

we stopped at a crossroads light,
emptiness everywhere but this rancho of cracked adobe,
chickens and a single goat.

In front of the corral,
a Mexican sat on a kitchen chair, his face tipped back
and bronzed like a mask.

We watched a young woman
trim his hair, then lean down for a whisper and a kiss,
their faces wrinkled with laughter,

making me ease the car ahead
to center and frame them in the open gate at our side,
while we waited for the light.

Your father turned
and watched them too, and though his face was shadowed,
I saw his features tighten and focus.

After the woman ran her fingers
through her husband's long dark hair and trimmed again,
your father closed his eyes and smiled.

Their voices came inside
but they never looked our way as we watched, oblivious
as a family photo

finished by a boy in a red bandana
entering from the right, chasing a black chicken
and making it fly.

Before we left that crossroads
with whatever it was we needed, the light went green
two or three times, I think.

Close

This house has lots of breathing space,
bathrooms to spare—
no need to look for the line of light
under that one door
that would keep me from barging in.
No bumping in the narrows
of the midnight hall, my father
sleepwalking past.
Yet some sound or mood of light
still puts me in that tiny house.
I can hear their nightly closeness.
I can listen to their dream
plans coming through thin walls
into the held breath of the hallway dark
before college made our house
look almost poor.
Those holidays home,
it is always late, too late in the kitchen.
Surprised, my mother lowers
her glass from view.
A moon fills the window behind her,
a red face looking in. My father
snores, just down the hall
in the bed that used to be mine.
Soon he will sleepwalk again,
moving farther away, drifting
into a breathless world beyond the stars.
In fact, he already has.
My mother and I sigh at the same time.
I watch her shuffle into the dim hall
toward a realm unreachably distant,
but still as close as air.

Against Distance

It was toward the end of the pier,
toward the shark rigs,
toward guys cracking beers and jokes
where fathers and kids used to fish all day,

I heard, then saw
    some forty yards off
a boy in a black tube caught fast in a rip tide,
waving an arm that couldn't be seen
by anyone, it seemed, but me.

In a few seconds, I knew,
he'd quit the tube and try for shore,
so I dove,
unable even later to remember
dropping my rod and reel,
removing sandals or climbing the rail,
seeing only the reflected arrow
of a body break the surface,
my lucky face
escaping a web of lines and hooks.

I swam toward something remembered,
the long shadow of Jack the Greek,
my uncle's buddy, breaking through
a quicksilver membrane,
his face pinched,
the arm reaching down, down,
to pluck me back into air.

I reached the boy
with just enough breath to blurt,
    "Stay with the tube,"
then over and over told him not to worry,
though I did

because the current was wicked and fast
and the pier hurried back and away.

Figures at the rail grew small,
and none I could see were running for help.

The valve stem bubbled hard
and boats I had seen from the pier
now disappeared.

Though he didn't cry,
his chin wrinkled like the stone of a peach,
his eyes grew huge,
    hazel and round,
a small worm scar on his cheek
scarlet from the sun,
my pep talk
doing little to soften all the taut
white lines of his face.

The clouds, mockingly,
swam at an easy pace toward the beach.

Never had I been so distant from shore
except in a boat,
and thought about the reef sharks
you often see around the end of the pier.
    "Don't splash," I said.

Besides, kicking was useless.
The rip would leave us far out when it quit.
The coast, at the top of swells, showed itself
    a long white line of sand,
a lime colored band of live oak and yaupon,
    and the beautiful faces of homes.

E. T. was his favorite film,
        baseball his favorite game.
His father lived in another town.
"Mom's under the pier with her friend."

Less than an hour ago
I had stood on the porch of our rental,
the sky all flickered white and torn with gull cries
over an ocean going from gloss to rough
where bait fish massed and mackerel sickled through
on a changing tide toward the pier.
I tapped the window, waved my arms,
pointed to the action,
did a dumb show of reeling like mad
but the kids,

enthralled by a video game,
were shadowy figures
drowning in an air-conditioned room,
glassed against the water and sand
with cartoon bombs detonating louder than the surf—
no interest in the older game
of cast and wait,
mackerel flanks all silver flecked with bronze.
So off I went with one of the five rods
I had just rigged
toward the long, tall pier in the distance.

No one was coming.
Moments got longer.
Water slapped at the tube.
The valve stem bubbled away.
And something sinister began.
A faraway house
alone on an undeveloped dune
        became a face
with wide apart dormers for eyes,

a porch-roof nose in between,
twin brick chimneys for ears.
The face, like some false god,
commanded belief, gloated,
then fixed us
with a sunstruck paneglass eye.
For a moment,
just a moment, I was ready to believe,
to sacrifice whatever it wanted,
until we drifted up to a raft
of gulls that rose and broke apart
like some selfish memory
I wanted to forget—
    an eighth-grade nun
who knew I'd come to no good end
for laughing always at the wrong time

as I did just then, a panicky cackle
that frightened the boy
who let go a cry, lonely and lost
as any I had ever heard, as if his mind
or mine had snapped,
then grew calm as the current.

At some point, unnoticed, the wind
turned about
and came at our backs with a push,
and kicking together, but so as not to splash,
we cheered ourselves, as the beach,
in glimpses at the top of swells,
    came slowly,
slowly closer, and that face
became a house again,

knots of tiny bathers below it,
and lone, dark figures bending for shells.

We kicked and rested.
Shouts and cries came over the surf
far from the pier
    where our toes touched sand again.
Children ran and dove, shellers stooped,
but no one arrived to wrap us
in blankets or hugs.
Unnoticed, we had been swept away.
The boy, shaking water, left his tube,
splashed from the shallows,
and ran toward the pier
where his mother
and the man who might one day be a father
returned to retrieve that leaky black tube
and look about
for another man now hidden
above them on the fishing pier.

    In the afterlife
of the cottage front room,
I lay on the sofa,
trying to focus that other world
within this one
wavering its magic light on the ceiling,
heavenly proof
of the buoyancy still in my limbs,
angels laughing around me
at sitcoms and game shows,
me drifting again,
air-conditioned as anyone,
thinking of saving
and of being saved

by a boy
who could have been my son
and kept me from drowning.

Ritual on Indian Pier

The pier was empty,
full of wooden groans,
the seas high,
the onshore drizzle
blowing horizontally.
I met a guy out here,
thin and old,
hollow in the temples,
a hook scar on his chin,
his ghostly face smiling
under a shaky lamp.

All night we fished,
outlasted everyone
through a long lull
that broke before dawn
with a school of blues.
Talk didn't matter
but when it came
his accent was shack poor
and hard to read.
That morning
at the cleaning table,
he noticed my hands
had never learned
to use a knife.

So he taught by gesture,
as if ashamed to speak,
spat on the white whetstone
and made small circles with the blade,
angling the steel,
honing an edge without feathers.
His black hand

would stop mine, guide it
in behind the gills to find the bone.
Toothless, he'd laugh,
then I'd watch his hand,
as if by magic,
in one motion, flip the fillet
and peel off the skin.
"Sharp knife do it all," he grinned,
holding the skeletal comb
to the x-ray light,
our ritual finished by gulls.

Tonight,
on the stone he made me keep
in exchange for a few beers, I find
the right angle,
make those same small circles.
His whole face smiled.
"Don't you worry," he said,
"time ain't nothin',"
and guided me through
every last blue,
laughing, covering his mouth,
then pursing his lips
as if kissing himself
or somebody else good-bye.
Years ago.
He must be dead by now.

As I cut these blues,
find the bone and work the knife,
his white whetstone
stands on the rail
against the dark,
like a marker finally set.

Leaning Against the Bar at Wrong-Way Corrigan's In Greenville, North Carolina

After James Wright

Over my head, I see the green toucan,
taunted into squawking, "Go for it!"
by a red-faced juicer with jesus hair and a pool cue.
Down two smoky stairs by the jukebox
pool balls follow one another
from the table's green field into long dark tunnels.
To my right,
on her bare shoulder, behind a scrim
of long bleached hair, a tattooed butterfly,
the color of crankcase oil, sleeps on and on.
I lean back, as the late news comes on overhead.
A drunk staggers out the door, blind for home.
I have wasted my cash.

Dust Devil

This was New London,
the first station with a rotating sign,
a bright orange SHELL,
and right after I had done six months
in produce at the A & P,
those fast building clouds,
the color of eggplant and endive.
I was gassing a Coupe de Ville
and down Coleman,
which was empty, comes this wind
you could see before hearing—

a twirling column of trash,
a drunk wobbling toward us
with a breathy roar
like the open door of a furnace
before it fell apart
under the big orange SHELL.
"Dust devil," I said, happy to name it.

The customer asked, "What was it?"
"Dust devil," I said again,
savoring the word,
wondering how such a dramatic self-
contained form could die so fast.
"I mean the *total*," he said.
"And catch the windshield, hunh?"
Still staring, I said I would.
"That'll be now, as in today, right?
I gotta make a meeting."

I fumbled coins
and counted change for a fifty,
(a lot of money then)

into his open palm,
as he puffed a cigar
and told me where he was headed,
then said: "Kid, do yourself a favor—
consider some other work."

I watched him disappear,
did myself the favor
of considering
the marvelous trash,
that gathering wind,
and the beautiful SHELL
slowly turning
against the churning eggplant
clouds about to cut loose.
Even then I knew
impatience was for amateurs,
for people with nothing
better to do than make a meeting
in Bridgeport.

Another Country

On the way to Guayaquil,
    still high in the Andes,
        stalled on a dirt road
    miles from a village,
we were cursing a tire
    for leaving us breathless,
        grease and dirt
    on our hands

when the hazy distance
    advanced a figure
        slowly more precise,
    a dark shape
dumpy as a cupcake
    but thick chested
        with a mountain
    of sticks on his back,
face thrust forward,
    tumpline to forehead.
        In black pants,
    he staggered,
straightening his load
    without stopping.
        Sandals slapping,
    he climbed steadily,
each breath a burst of air,
    the curve taking him
        out of sight, leaving us
    looking at dark spots
of sweat in the dust.

Then higher up,
     that mountain of sticks
         floated left to right
     above the tropical florescence
past tilled horizontal rows,
     on vertical slopes,
         up switchbacks fading
     into a region of clouds,
some promise of sleep.

Sometimes when I need him,
that man in sandals
wobbles into sight
through veils of heat,
his breath roaring
like a fire,
wood clacking on his back,
that bronze Incan face,
the load-bearing step
that moves
into a thickening dark.

Fluteman

There's a dirt road that goes deep
    into high desert,
and this time I want to go deeper, further past Price,
into the ancient quiet of Nine Mile Canyon.
It's a lumpy brown sugar trail, sweeter and sweeter
the further it goes
past the remains of a mining town,
ghost rails rusting in sage,
glass chips glinting in the weeds,
    then narrowing
between sandstone walls of light siennas
and dark umbers getting higher.

None of our everyday gab and gimme—
only the sandrock glyphs of the Fremonts
who have held their tongues for a thousand years.
The road peters out
so I leave the Jeep, its clever built-in compass,
and trust my feet.
The last safe sound is metal creaking in the heat
quickly lost to the thunder
    of mere footfalls
and the roar of continuous breath
on a steep climb far above the valley floor
in the sweating sun toward
    a ten-foot snake
    and a perfect lizard,
bright orange, peened out of black desert varnish.

Just under foot, darting into a crevice,
the same lizard that served as a model
makes you wonder about the snake
and careful where you place your feet.

Along the ledge are images of ladders,
    hands and faces,
    spirals, spiders, and deer—
mule deer that still graze the wild grasses
far below in the sun
that heats my hatless head
with a crazy feeling
small hunters could be back any second
to reclaim these caves and ledges.
    A head-dressed bow hunter
    or a dark man dipped in varnish,
using a deerbone tool
to peck these totems that blaze out in orange
through a blue-black glaze on the rockface.
    Around the corner,
a child, a woman, and woodsmoke,

but that's the oven sun,
and loss of fluid
so I take the chance
(though there is no path)
of an easier way down through the shade
of cottonwoods hugging the cliff
and come face to face
with a man in a darkened alcove,
a stick figure in a square-topped hat
arms extended, but crooked for the flute
he must have played right here
in this echo chamber, bent back perhaps
in the ecstasy of a high note.

I sit for a moment to rest and listen.
    A rockchuck yelps.
Then the canyon breathes
as he plays the land
through a deerbone flute

two, three, four notes
of perfect pitch, the last
held long, then fading
into the breath of the canyon,
a resonant hum drawn out
over rimrock
same color as the sun going down.

Valentine

Did I ever tell you that years ago I escaped
the icy sidewalks and falling snow to buy my first

for a girl named Judy? In Kresge's five-and-dime?
Early dark made the front windows into slabs of black,

so with card in hand, I drifted down the aisle
to my favorite spot past the pink lingerie, and dreamed

at a tank teeming with goldfish, watching them
spurt and glide, balance perfectly still, before facing

that brittle outside dark again. Oh, don't worry,
you'll have chocolate, and roses too, but remember

how once, windward of the jetty, we lost the engine?
I drop the anchor quick but those quarry rocks,

blacker for the sun and pale blue water, keep coming
closer and closer. My eyes race down the rope

through thirty feet of water clear as dreamfright
to where the anchor flukes are plowing the bottom,

then catch on coral, halting those ragged black rocks
only ten feet from our hull. Then it was you

who lifted the cowl, found where the coil
wire frayed, and gave us fire again.

So we lingered, engine idling, to watch beneath the boat
a huge school of spade fish shaped and striped

like those french angels our son used to have in his tank.
Suddenly they were gone.

Which is to say, you always take me back
to teenage gold and the primary colors

of coral and communal fish, that pale blue
water on which our down-looking faces float,

slide into each other and eclipse,
as in a dream—one more way

that we merge, rarely guessing how often we drift
into, away from, around, and through.

Distance at the Dockside Inn

Diners under blue awnings turn
to watch a two-masted ketch in the channel,
burnished by a low sun. This is the moment
you notice the one person
who hasn't turned, the moment
halyards stop slapping their masts,
her body bent forward, the shoulders bobbing,
her face twisted with tears, the moment
everything is straining to hear
those shouts, cries, and whispers deep inside
a story that is always the same.

The man at the table leans forward,
touching her shoulder, but much too late.
The diners look, then look at their glasses of wine,
the faultless sun, a far-off sail by Monet.
Her torso nods in time
to the waves from a careless runabout.
Across the channel, just above her shoulders,
two wild horses come down the dune
to the eelgrass shallows, one following the other
along a shelf of hard sand
into a perfect red circle of sun.

A Guide to Arrival

All the way to heaven is heaven
—St. Catherine of Siena

Remove your watch
and pick a place,
the back porch, say.
Expect nothing
when you step out

toward the blue crowns
of hydrangea that draw
attention to the absence
of wind.

Sit on the steps.
Watch the yard
shed its dark colors,
and dogwood tire
of its white meaning.

Don't think
that flicker in the oak
is a May Day
from childhood,
some S.O.S. from the past.
No past at all.

The cat sheds fur
that floats from your hand
like milkweed fluff.

Absorb the stillness,
however momentary,
as if in a photo,

followed by a bird cry
not dying away.

In slow motion steps,
the cat takes
her patchwork fur
and vanishes
into the patchwork shade.
You say her name
but she won't come back.

What else do you want?
Tell yourself nothing
that's not right here,
leaves bursting into light,
light into leaves.

Trafficking with Voices

Tired of talk,
I lowered the headset volume
and instead gave in to the endless mantra
of the single engine Cherokee Arrow.
My friend Ed kept tabs on the instruments,
listened to distant men and women
who moved us from sector to sector
and told him what to do.

I quit looking
at tiny houses, rivers,
and yellow buses full of kids headed home.
Older voices whispered like white sound,
white as the sacred mountains
of the book in my lap.
When I looked up later
from Himalayan peaks on the page,
the towering clouds all around seemed right.

Then specks appeared on the storm scope,
swarms of amber bees due south.
"I know," said Ed. He talked to McGuire Control
while I watched the clouds ahead,
not white any more with azure escapes.
Threads of lightning
stitched them tighter and blacker.

On instruments, you can't climb
until they tell you to, as in Simon Says,
so we waited right into the front
and the sun went out like a bulb.
The book shot from my lap
and hit the cockpit roof. The wings flexed,
and rain crackled like flung gravel.

All dark,
except for the instruments, lightning,
and the whites of Ed's eyes as he worked
to keep control. I thought of the outer
dark from inside its turbulence

and down the aisle, for no reason
I could think of quite,
strode Sister Paulita in the 5th grade,
yanking me from my seat so hard
that my eyeballs rattled
like dice in a black leather cup.
No luck. I was ready for the outer dark
of that freezing New England fire escape
for sneaks, gigglers and cutups
when I heard
the voice of an improbable poem:

Cherokee Triple Seven Zero Delta,
this is McGuire Control,
climb to ten thousand feet
on a heading of one six niner
and stand by for a new vector home.

Later, racing with the moon,
way up in the midnight blue,
me humming that old tune by Vaughn Monroe,
Ed asked what I'd found so funny
down in that storm.
"Remember the nuns?" I said.
"How you had to sing alone,
how they'd shake the hell out of you,
how lucky it felt to be heading home after school?"

"We had the brothers," he said,
"now they call it child abuse."
And we laughed like guilty kids again.

Far below our starboard wing,
by itself in a vast space, its nav lights blinking,
a small plane like ours
slowly sank into a bank of clouds that flashed,
every so often, like a broken neon tube.

That lucent voice, almost sourceless, I thought,
and hoped it was talking them through.

from
**The Sunken Lightship
(1990)**

Story of a Sound

It begins in the vestry
with a customary two dollar bill
from groom to servers.
    My first wedding,
a scent of wine from cut glass cruets—
the same burgundy
color as the kneeler cushions
where they wait for their names
from the priest:
"Dominic Trancreda . . . Carmella Peronne . . . ."

Her bridal veil is lifted,
a small yellow stain on the bodice,
the face pale,
a beauty mark above her parted lips . . .
"Do you, Carmella, take . . . ."
Looking at me, she lowers her eyes
and the silence stretches to a yes.

That night, the newspaper says
her husband, a dent in the middle
of his heavy chin, is a butcher.
I clip her photo, carry her heart-
shaped face for months
behind the veil,
as if in a cocoon,
lips the color of a cherry
that tops the sundae
I'm famished for. Then, whispering
Carmella, Carmella,
I taste the sound
that deepens everything I see.

She wants
to live a certain kind of life
away from the block and cleaver,
that hateful apron smeared with blood,
her voice urging,
Do it for me, Carmella,
that name in the dark room turning
the barrel of a portrait lens—
Carmella at the altar of sleep
lovelier than any Madonna,
giving her name to my lips
even when awake.

Carmella.
I'm twelve,
married for the first time
to a name.

Answering Voices

We address an emptiness in the street
or in the mute space of a journal,
puzzling with the sounds that we hear.
Inside is where they sleep
or come at waking
from a sphere we barely believe in.
Angels of welcome,
they beg for response,
invite a self to sound itself out.

Imperative, they throb into being,
the language as plain as a mother's.
Shhh, your father's asleep.
Or the nearly forgotten
pitch and rhythm of an old priest:
Pater noster qui es in cælis . . . .
Dead language
brought back to life.
And we have answered the angels.

Lips moving, caught in the act,
our faces crimson, still
we carry on with punch-lines,
bookish abstractions,
the vulgate figures of friends,
whatever serves
this odd process of oxygenation,
a motion that carries toxin from the blood,
inflates the half-filled lung.

A moon floats over the trees,
round and bright as a new Spalding:
Fork your fingers on the stitches.

It's my uncle's voice,
ragged with tobacco and vodka.
Alone, we are never alone.

Brothers of the Double Life

Love is basically a suspension of gravity.
            —Don DeLillo

Against the wind and rain, the house
makes odd sounds as if trying to be still.
The invisible is all around us, you once joked,
but thin air has been your home
for nearly a year.

Air, even and steady, a bright chain rising
from the tiny diver in my son's aquarium, safe
from the stormy light that makes
everything something else—those pillows
a body, that shoe a rat.
        The aquarium glows,
a calm green lamp of magnification.

Today, small craft warnings
and to be out at the reef would be a bad dream,
but in other weather, gung-ho for grouper,
we drifted live bait from first light,
        from reef to the tanker wreck.
And the Carolina coast showed off
as if it knew you were from up north
and didn't have long
to take in the fantasia of pink and pearl clouds
and April fragrance
        that the land breathed out all morning.

Makos often fin the wreck
        but this day it was dolphin.
Eyes so keen, they were in
        and out of our lines, never fooled,
playing, without ever grazing a bait.

Or causing a reel to click even once,
water clear to fifty feet down
where, half-hidden by its white-spotted mama,
a calf synchronized its swimming to hers.

Never had I seen so many this close.
As if needed, here they were,
come to the rescue, near enough to pet,
you leaning over the bow, dipping a hand
as if such water could cure
divorce, lost children, parents recently dead.
But watching was enough,
the quick caper and flurry
that elongates and launches those great smilers,
high in the air where they hang
before becoming wholly water again.

Perfect, like the clarity
of my son's aquarium, where lyre-tail,
pearl and pink gourami
slowly turn, or hang weightless as dreams—
a reminder of what you never were,
weightless, always running, biking,
training your body to be less and less.
And now it's gone, it's air
like the dolphin you leaned toward,
just out of reach, untouchable,
mysterious as the future,
the dolphin I count on
to swim me to sleep.

Waterlight ripples on the white plaster wall.
The invisible presses
with a lowering sky,
    the line squall that drove us into port
then home along a rainy road,

    still seeing those dolphin,
yet unequal to what we saw,
reduced to a beer and a wise joke
about how we would never again take the bait.

But more like sharks than dolphin,
we do take the bait, move forward to breathe,
the dead living in us
as we breathe them into a future
of perfect moments, like this one
before the aquarium that reminds us
of radiance and grace.
We watch from the world of air,
haunted by the green inner calm,
always hoping it will dream us again.

    in memoriam Bernard Meredith

A Sense of the Other Side

Back home at last
after seeing my mother
lowered into frozen earth,
I couldn't find sleep
with wine or even pills,
when our calico, as if
called, came to the sofa
and did something
never repeated since—

One soft foot at a time,
she climbed on my chest,
looked through the blank
lid of my face, made
the faintest cry, then
curled over my heart
and slept, so that I could,
for three nights in a row—
visitations like belief,
unreal, against all odds.

Catlight

There is so little that is close and warm
                    —Wallace Stevens

Cats won't perform.
        They make you perform.
So here you are, playing
        Master of the Back Door,
powerless, feeling the winter
        freeze and the dark
that suggests—but just then
        a touch of white.

From the dark depths,
        in no hurry, she comes,
nonchalant across the lawn,
        under the car,
stopping to scratch an ear,
        then sits and stares,
while you attend the door
        and babytalk
to the backyard until she decides
        it's time.

Nose still wet and cold, she
        presents herself
to your lap, the gift she knows
        you know she is,
and takes you from trivia,
        TV news, some article
you recall about cats
        spending two thirds
of their lives asleep, or at rest.

Your fingers, drunk on her fur,
	forget that tabled wineglass
and slip over the patchwork of black,
	white, and the rust
that turns to *café au lait* when you pet
	against the grain.

And the exquisite whiskers, her skull
	like a kneecap, that mouth,
like a snake's when she yawns,
	which is often,
then the tickling rasp of her tongue.

Drowsing, she purrs her one mantra
	while the left ear
independently tracks a kid
	peeling rubber in the street.
Her one cracked eye is a vote
	for dynamic stillness.

	Yes, you say, and mumble
about Eastern Thought, immobility,
	Pascal and *divertissement.*

But like one of your students,
	she yawns again,
for you're such a slow learner—
	she's so tired
of teaching you stillness,
	nonchalance,
how to care while seeming not to,
	sleeping
so that you might,
	as in rare moments like this,
dream wide awake,
	making all things live
in vivid, unusual light, catlight.

Equations

The lights flicker and the kitchen
disappears until my mother comes back
with a hurricane lamp, determined
that a blackout won't keep me from homework.

Everything is still but the wind
and the steady gas breath of the oven
where the bread keeps rising,
the scent of yeast and nutmeg spreading.

My father is at work in the shipyard.
And every school night of this rainy winter
in the year of Sister Scholastica's scowl
my mother helps me with impossible math.

Let x equal the moment
that the power fails, as if Nazis
have zeroed in on the light above tabled books
and my mother's selfless ambitions.

And y the way space shrinks
and draws so comfortably close
that the shove and slug of the playground
disappear with the granite church:

x plus y plus the bright water
of her eyes where I see myself
suspended, dark and tiny, but in fine detail,
held intact, ready at last to respond.

Heaven

The mobiles he made of broken pane-
glass, tin, or brass piping
always touched off tunes
under the front and back porch eaves.

Every tree had a house for the right bird.
Gourds for purple martins
hung from a wire between distant trees
and looked like whole notes against the sky.

The cellar was where he did his making.
I learned to size nails, love the everlasting balm
of paint, the clean scent of soft pine
and sanded oak, the good smell of sweat,
the look of sawdust
like a pile of gold filings under his vise.

   My mother gone,
he quit the Church, after years of Mass.
But the brass touchings of his chimes
are matins that take me
through the cold crisis of waking
moment by moment.
Sawdust is a sermon.
Birdcries are *Kyries*.
My father built a heaven about my ears.

Stephen Judy's Execution

His face fills the screen,
famous a little longer for its smile
and canine teeth, big like mine.

He looks beyond the camera
at all the late-night drinkers and snackers,
without remorse, determined to die.

Pitiless, he smiles.
Cut to a room, all bars and shadows
where death has built a chair, hard and simple,
a future for itself.

Judy grins.
My armchair gives a jolt.

                    *

I leave the house,
a country I no longer love.

The moon advertises a better life.
One by one, streets and sleeping windows fall
behind, arguments for and against.

I come to a fence, a wide tobacco field.
One light in a tenant shack,
far on the other side.
A man with a cigarette perhaps,
plotting a future, his lungs feeding on dreams
of profit and loss.

                    *

The quarter moon
smiles sharply at a life with others.

There's a point in Defoe's island book
where Crusoe contemplates the reef and the new wreck
and realizes that one man's safety
is another man's destruction.

Or an animal's perhaps.
The fox I shotgunned in the yard once: rabies,
a red plot against the snow, something or other.
That night I wasn't safe. Barely tamed,
my hands lay like animals at my sides.

        *

Judy's foster mother begged
he be kept alive and studied . . . .

The smallest cells, lethal genes, the secret
circuitry of his behavior
all beg to be understood.

The night's electric blue.
                    Past Saturn
a probe moves us to the fringes of what we know.

I stand here watching the light in that shack.
Everything is reduced to that one light.
Warm, yellow, alive, and oddly poignant
across the field. Suddenly
there's darkness where it was.

Historic Present

(Loire Valley, 1975)

Blois, Chambord, Amboise, and then
the road again, distance
arranging farmscapes in the windshield.

God, let something astonishing arrive
to erase sharp words,
the Peugot's flat, a son's anger.

Dates, the mythic details
of famous lives, fact and motive
ask for mastery, promise answers

that down the road might matter.
De Medici, De Guise, François I—
who did what to whom and when

in these regal but impossible plots?
Only the general suffices:
power, jealousy, betrayal of love.

A wife and son ice me with looks.
Once wanted, information taunts like
royal emblems—boar and porcupine:

Ne me touchez pas. And the rain
relents, as if ordered, giving us
a night in some small town, nameless now.

After dinner my family goes to bed.
I take a walk, too full
of good food and helpless history.

Who was it, freshly stuffed with truffles,
went to see Huguenots
dance themselves blue in the noose?

I even forget where da Vinci died, but
never this summer night,
nor the crimson hearts of poppies

blooming along the path that stops dead
at the riverbank and turns inward:
I see a palace chamber, an open casement

brilliant with moonlight, a poster bed.
My queen, my young blond prince
still sleep in this fragile light.

Valluris: Café des Voyageurs

At red metal tables
we rest outside over beers
and appraise what we've seen
in the low slanting light.
There are palm trees,
but this is no paradise.
The past is expensive.
Our legs are dumb from walking.
A blue wall protects us
from a wind as stubborn as want.

Our son climbs
with a dark-haired boy
on the plinth of the "Goat-herd"
Picasso made for the square.
They hug its bronze legs
and turn about
where merchants on Sunday morning
pile the newspaper
to wrap their flowers and fish—
a fresh indifference to art,
to dates in the *Michelin,*
and the Roman ruins nearby.

Running and laughing,
our son chases pigeons again.
They land and scatter.
We watch them circle,
gust in the wind
over roofs tilting
toward some other haven,
something lost
always longing
to be found.

Navajo Land

Hogans and beat-up trucks,
roadside ramadas,
dustdevils, sandstone and silence.
And between the canyon rims
it's wall to wall blue overhead,
the same bits of sky
you see on the belts,
fingers, and necks of these first people.

High in the desert
under such a wide sky,
there are no small moments.
In dry air hot as a sauna
that pigmy juniper
might as well be a redwood.
And the sun
is a fiery spider
knitting its filaments
as in the petroglyph
we saw from horseback
at the trailhead.
Oblivion has not yet seen to them,
these "old ones,"
and next to a tongue
of soot from a campfire
in the tenth century
we see their thoughts
figured in red rock—
hand, lizard, scorpion, deer—
reminders of a seeing so pure
it begs for rebirth.
But this is romance too.
My native guide,
more up to date than I,

more interested in Larry Bird
and the NBA
than the ancient quail
carved in the sandstone
above his horse,
wants to trade
turquoise and silver
for my son's Celtic's hat
with a plastic adjustable band

*

We hike
to the beds of dinosaurs
where scholars came to read the bones
and puzzle out the body
architecture of great animals
gone but for the three-toed prints
that lope to the edge of the canyon rim
and into the deep dry air,
prints made too long ago even to imagine
or make sense of,
but later at a skeletal ramada
I see how we make what we need—
silver, turquoise, and jade,
jewelry on velvet black as a wild night sky
above the mesa.

A raven floats over.
"Nothing around here," says the Navajo boy,
"but rattlers and jackrabbits."

And the ageless glyphs of the Anasazi:
sun, quail, spider,
scorpion, turtle, deer.

Raven, Mountain, Snow

It's the after-Christmas blue
of snow in high country, our cabin
broken into and looted, ravens
in the Ponderosa, a mocking crew.

Glass swept, I work my way
along the mesa rim on a snow crust
that breaks and puts me up to my waist
in the mockery of ravens again.

And the three distant peaks,
mountains first sacred to the Hopi,
are scarred with ski runs
clear-cut through fir and spruce.

But the air is cold and pure.
And all the Zen props are in place—
mountain, snow, and pine—
to remind me

of the Rinpoche to the novice:
You must place a ladder
against the pear tree
so the thief won't break his leg.

Three heavy ravens give up,
caw less at the nothing I need to flee.
Rung by rung, afternoon descends
in the bright fading colors of a bruise.

Phantoms at Swan Quarter

There is nothing old in America save the forests . . .
that is, in itself, worth many a monument and ancestor.
                                        —Chateaubriand

All through the inside weather of winter, our storms
        and freezes, I fold, unfold the chart,
an eye to the pale blue seas at sister islands
        that want us to find what is there.

We chug through a maze of brushy meanders.
        Noon heat and the motor's threat
send a moccasin from its eelgrass blind—a watery
        cursive that says it was here.

Past the barnacled carcass of an oyster boat,
        the water opens a smooth new sheet.
We pick up speed on a dead reckon across the bay,
        red nuns nodding astern

as now we make for the Judith Narrows, veering
        from an Ocracoke ferry that falls
to port, its bridge above the marsh grass fading
        like a French cathedral in favor

of the first bars of an unknown bird that takes
        the place of the motor when I kill it.
But the bird flees, hides a shy blue before our book
        can give it a name. An osprey whistles

and dives, redwings flit through cattails, stronger
        for their whispered names. On cushions
we stretch out, yield to a current, let our bodies
        play Adam and Eve, taste the deep salt,

feel the hot-towel press of the sun—witness
        our only act. Bread, good brie,
a bottle of white Papillion. Even the landmark
        tower, red across the bay, won't quite

become a nick on the wide water under clouds
        that invent themselves, billow,
and darken. Light is never the same. Brown rays,
        mating, fin the surface like sharks

as they circle, then bank in formation, delta wings
        in clear water under the boat before
three olive Phantoms streak in, screaming at wargames
        so low we can see helmets that give us

the high sign and send every bird in the refuge
        clattering up to darken the air
like battle smoke, the settlement slow and sadly changed,
        with an old dream of the motor

not starting, the squall quickly on us. Or the dream
        motor starting on its own, dragging us back
into winter, with no memory, only the map, the blues
        fading, as if we had never been here.

Part of a Story

Outside that predawn diner
was a moment
outside every moment I ever spent
with my father on that truck.
Bird voices, soft as honey,
dropped through leaves in the dark.
Listen, he said,
to what he first heard on the farm,
dove murmurs, some story told by his mother.
But I ached to be old
enough to be a driver like him
awake while the world slept,
tough enough to glug down coffee, hot,
and make the waitress laugh
with stories of my own.

What was that story
about doves, their sorrowful
notes falling like ripe fruit?
I forget.
I forget everything
but us being outside
and his being outside
of himself and taking time
to tell it in the quiet
while hard hours
of blacktop waited, me
getting antsy for speed
and a chance to drive,
the east getting brassy already.

These many years later,
up before dawn
with the trucker I wanted to be,

the dark dream fading,
I wait for the coffee to perk,
on the way to my desk, that dove
mourning outside in the eaves,
across the years to another
above the distant wheeze
of diesels idling
dark under trees.

Reflections on a Likeness of Luke

Ceci n'est pas une pipe.
        —Réné Magritte

This isn't Luke.
It reveals an obsession with Luke.

Luke had a mole, right here.
This is Luke.

It's a dream image of Luke.
It's Luke dreaming of a better image.

It shows a shotgun, not a guitar.
It's the guy who robbed the Zip Mart.

It shows the Luke in all of us.
It's a Luke-type look-alike, kind of.

It's a mask haunted by others.
It's the lonely self haunted by its own mask.

It's a woman posing as Luke.
It's Luke posing as himself, unsuccessfully.

This can't be Luke.
It's a lie that reveals the true Luke.

It's the only Luke of its kind.
It's more real, more knowable than Luke.

It's Luke mythologized.
It's Luke deconstructed.

It's Luke new-historicized.
It's Luke post-modernized.

It's happy and sad, deep and shallow—
It squints the viewer, reads the reader.

from
Where We Live
(1982)

Binoculars

At Midway
my uncle filled them
with kamikazes, boas of smoke, flakpuff
and a sky full of Hollywood flames.

War over,
he gave those heavy tubes to me,
"The little Marine,"
for backyard battles with playmates.

At night,
hooded like a great hawk,
they perched on my tall bureau
resting from the hours I would move

what I wanted
in and out of their bright sharp circles,
then dive for cover, like Uncle, a gunner
mad for movement, magnification.

Carelessly
I filled them with anything
and envied how they enlarged and then forgot
the choppy lake, stone sky, and how

Uncle fired
over trees at a formation of ghost fighters
and followed one peeling off, bearing in,
to bang down a mallard.

I watched
squirrels and pheasants fall in the lenses
and Mrs. Daniels undressing at night
until my eyeballs throbbed at the root.

At the track
I learned to focus "fillies" in the stands
then swing the horses, liquefied with speed,
into dark tunnels beating with blood.

Now they dangle,
twist on a cracked leather strap from a coat-tree,
and stare at the floor for days,
as if in a VA ward, not wanting to focus.

Dziadek

Off Route 44
a dusty road winds back
to an abandoned farm
(like Dziadek's)
assaulted by briar and weeds
and going back to the land.

Only highschoolers come out here
to park
and nightly shed their skins
that wither in the dust
under white July suns.
But I have come to take photos
to find a way of seeing the farm.

When he died
they came from three states,
dutifully, in winter.
Smoke in the closed car
burned my eyes
as we waited for the priest
at the graveyard
and my aunt told how he chose
the suit he would wear
and the prayers he wanted said.
The Sobieski Knights,
men of the same soil,
shivered, threw sods,
then left for different farms.

How shall I frame it?
Through blurred daisies and stems?
There must be a way
to capture, to hold the color

of heat in these fields,
but within me it is black and white
and cold
and snowing past parlor windows
where Dziadek lies
yet leads me away
from weeping aunts and drinking uncles
to see the cows that heat the barn
with the heavy raw smell of their bodies
as they stand and chew,
mouths dangling silver threads of saliva.
Krowa, comes his raspy rattling whisper.
Krowa, I say after him
and touch the rough hair of its face.
My hand winces and he laughs.

I sit deep in clover,
sight the barn through
fuzzed, slender reeds of grass.
It leans out of plumb,
broken-slatted and baring
its wooden bones to the wind.

Once again, snapped tangent
to the rusty gutted pick-up,
thin vertical lines of sun
burn between its shrunken
dark-grained boards, precisely

like the barn where I went
to be bitter and alone
because the priest was late,
because my eyes still burned,
(but not from smoke)
and the priest had read the wrong prayer.

Krowa, I say as I circle the house.
Krowa, a word that breaks off a bit
of the farm and Dziadek,
the whisper, the white mustache
and his brown-toothed laugh.
Krowa. The relic of an *ethos*
I have glimpsed and my children
will never know.

I am walking through
shadowy empty rooms,
the walls peeling faded floral paper,
chunks of plaster and its fine
white dust. Shadows and the hot
dry smell of rot make a squirm
at the pit of my gut. *Krowa*, I mouth it
like a prayer.

I come upon a frame of light
and aim through the broken pane
that gives on wild roses, breeze-tossed,
scratching upon the house.
Now I shoot, the pane out of focus,
and focus on the rose
and suddenly I have found
what is meant by aiming out.

Standing in the keep-deep grass,
I frame the house this one last time
so as not to forget.
I whisper *krowa, Dziadek*.
The cows are still chewing
and Dziadek takes my hand.

Witness

after a photo in The Best of LIFE

Faces that encircle
the boy and the fox
encircled a small woods

and moved the game
to this field of snow
cropped and tense,

black and white,
shaped by an idea
of time and space—

Holmes County, Ohio,
where a fox is cornered,
panting on black legs.

The tongue dangles
like a rag. Back legs
buckle; it squats

and squirts the snow
with terrified piss.
It does not see

the club, the boy
hatted like a batter
with a Little League grin.

His last two swings
have made two foxes
stiffen on the ground

like exclamation points
at his feet. No shadows.
The sun is elsewhere.

Family faces, expectant.
Smiles, mute cheers—
all behind him.

It is time; he steps
cautiously forward
like the crowd's one wish

cocking his long stick
in this paper place
of primal black

and white
where we must gather again
and again.

The Commons

They are changing its look.
A bulldozer pierces its skin,
noses in red depression

and mows down trees at the edge.
A crane comes up
with jawfuls of earth, the stump

and dangling roots of an oak—
an image of Saturn
fisting his half-eaten child.

A rust wind blows at dusk
from the diggings, dirt sifting
back. There is nothing to help.

In our daydreams
or the flickerings of deep sleep,
The Commons will never change:

the bell is ringing,
we gather in the sun,
the rifles are about to speak

May 4, 1970
Kent State University

Hunger

Next to his shack, my neighbor hangs
an eight-point buck by the hind legs.
It dangles from an apple bough
in this white papery air between us.
I tell him I used to trap
muskrat, mink, otter, and coon—coon when
all the kids were randy for Crockett hats
and ringtails brought as much money as mink.

Behind his flensing knife,
the beige hide gives way to red meat,
his muddy yard to my father's garage:
a muskrat hangs from the beam, nearly naked,
its fur pulled inside out
like a bloody glove on my hand,
newspaper spread at my feet.
I'm fast, I never make holes in a pelt.

He smiles at me like an old buddy
but a blade is between us, a carcass, and
something else. Rifles bark in the hills.
He smiles a demented smile.
I quicken like a dog, stiffen.
At the back of my mind, a cold garage.
A wild season begins and blood-flowers,
one at a time, then clusters,
bloom through the newspaper print.

Meat

I

In his old-country beard, your grandfather
blessed himself, a steaming tub in the background.
You see the barn-beam, the pulley and rope
and the eye-level pig twisting before
that autumn knife shaped like a ritual scream.

II

The cowpoke squints (his cheek a tumor of tobacco)
and electrically prods the endless steers
up a wooden ramp to the first specialist
on the disassembly line of this long factory.
They call him 'the killer" and, armed with electrodes,
he shocks the bellowing beast to its short knees,
as the metal door flings open and, end over end,
it falls into a hot red light where a hoister
chains a hind leg and up kicking, wide-eyed and
upside down, it takes a clanking overhead tram
to the gum-chewing throat-cutter. See
how he uses the special hooked knife to get that bright
spurt and spray on rubber boots and apron. See
how the white-suited slitters joke and wait
for bellies while stropping their blades. See

how the cavity-men lean in to unpack that
hot rank case, root with a sharp right hand
and turn with armfuls of gutflop: lungs and
liver, kidneys, glands, the still-wincing
heart, mucus, silver plop and slither. See
how the conveyor men, earphoned against clank and
roar, watch football in four tubes along the line
and let their hands go down and out and in—

a pattern of cut and lift, sometimes a squint
at the tripe, a wish for the gold watch
that might have been swallowed. But on to the saw-
men who make the sides (with a high motorized whine),
the skinners, drapers, heavers and haulers, inspectors,
heapers of hides, boilers of gristle, packers and
shippers—God loves them all, as He does the ears
and tails, boilings and try-outs, crimson floor tides,
the drain-suck, the bone, the shit, and the bristle.

Workin' Construction

Good hefty words.
Easier than mixing mortar
and shouldering bricks up ladders
that made those college summers
ache for the first two weeks
or more.

That phrase
meant money, muscle, a deep tan,
shots and beers—nothing
like the light of words
I couldn't find at night, drunk
with fatigue on my parents' back porch,
fireflies fading
        one by one
like bits of the day.

It took me a whole summer to read one thin book.

Mornings, back I went
to dizzy smells of mortar and firsap,
cardboard and creosote,
the sight of girders going up and
welders hunched over torches and violet flickers
binding great steel frames of sky.

By the end of summer
our brick tiers took us above the town
I saw whole and sadly small
for the first time, bordered by river,
rusty bridge, and walling hills.

        Below me
it all begs for focus.

The whistle blows.

The masons snap clean their trowels.
Jaw and joke.

   And hand over hand
I talk myself down to the ache and smell,
trying to get the feeling
that will please me
as working construction once did.

My Son Draws an Apple Tree

I watch it grow
at the end of his dimpled hand
rooted in white paper.

The strokes are fast
and careless, as if the hand
had little time.

Quick black trunk,
a green crown and in the white
air all by itself

a red splotch,
an apple face with a frown
that is his

he gravely says
looking up at me—the stiffening
branch he falls from.

Hang-glider

. . . le travail imbécile de chaque jour
                                      —Albert Camus

I saw you, a bright red stain
blown against the huge cliffs
behind our house. Sullen climbers
from the village gendarmerie
lowered that broken body,
slumped in a yellow rope net.

You died all day and night but
still soar in our marrow and blood.
I see a shadow fly on the snow
before the hum and high whistle and
red kite panel slide above us
with a dangle of legs and skis.

You cock back my head with
another pass, hanging from wires
and bright fabric, a helmet and
goggles—no face. You must be
hiding from your wife. But why?
I've see her often in the street—

young, blond, beautiful, looking up
as if your red kite panel might suddenly
appear, slowly circling the summit.
But who is it for? This graceful
handling of winds that keeps
the valley from blowing away?

Neighbors hate you—wires full of
that tangled, high-pitched whisper
driving dogs to howl and leap.

Now it is quiet; the stain is gone.
And I know what to think: no man
with a wife and two children . . .

C'est la connerie . . . not courage.
I know, I know. But there you are
in a sky hungry for color, staying up,
fabric straining, wires sending
some inaudible message to dogs
that howl and leap at our fences.

Southern Snow

It transforms the street and yard,
rends us by being rare. Still stiff with sleep,
we watch our son jump off the porch, disappear
with no memory of wet wool, snow
down the neck. The furnace shivers on.
He dives into a drift, rolls, laughs with a friend.
Does skin touching snow still burn like an angel's?

We are walkers again. Morning's pure resurrection.
Offices closed, we help our neighbors dig out.
We talk. And with no cars to blur the streets
our listening carries us farther than ever.

Tonight more snow. And slowly an unbearable
sameness. A garage caves in with the weight.
Miz Keel's spotted hand turns brittle pictures
of the only time this happened before: 1929,
Ford Model A's all mounded high, impounded.
Men in fedoras clown and pose with snowmen
teaching us how to live with the whiteness
two more days. Was their laughter really delight?

Weeks from now, at the end of stiff rainy days,
wild crab tree petals, as a kind of revenge,
will fill the air, whiten the vigorous grass
and those lost moments will burn again, like snow.

Rerun Scene: You Rescue My Son

The river is fast and black and theatrically high.
Chest-deep, you strain, lean against the current.

You hand me up Keith, dripping and cough-crying
from the fast black river I've climbed from.

I run him breathless to the house, bone-cold, blue,
hurry him into a hot bath. The skin, numb, stings

back to feeling. The mud-stink leaves but clings.
The water is fast and black and theatrically high.

We act, minimize to his mother, but all afternoon
he's a little red jacket sweeping down and away.

The TV flickers, booms with a Bowl Game that
barely reaches the fast black water with heros.

American, cowboy-laconic, we accept the drumming
of December rain as ironic applause. You lean,

seem pleased to be straining; you lift him, crying
from the fast black water, giving him back forever,

a sweet mad thanks between us, assumed but unsayable
except in dreams or rerun scenes like this.

for Mike Strada

Teachers

Some odd revolution, Mr. Pasquale, has brought you back
destroying time and space to get here. It's afternoon

after your lecture on the Era of Revolution and you are
chewing me out. You remove your glasses, your dark face

disgusted that I'm merely taking up space, wasting time,
saying, *Makuck, if breath weren't involuntary, you'd be dead!*

Time, space, and breath. You have none of those now
except as I give them to you here and watch you get lost

in Revolution, Rochambeau, Louis-Philipe, and miss
the revolution of heads to the back row as our own Philip

Greenwood unzips, brandishes himself in honor of the fallen
Bastille, or something. Giggles bring you back, glasses on,

angry, toppled. But time, Mr. P., should allow us to laugh
at reversals. This is the Space Age, it's okay to be spacey—look

at this probe to reach you. And my watching the clock's more
refined, almost an art. But I'm here to praise, not curse you,

for coming back from an awful nowhere, for no reason
except, perhaps, to help celebrate ironies and odd revolutions.

Back Roads By Night

A need for it grows—not the white-knuckle stuff
with second-gear rubber, racing for a case of beer,
dusting some kidface with a hot Chevy. I mean:
that first time I soloed in my father's car
I drove for hours, slowly, through state forest—
a gullet of darkness ribbed out with trees.

A deer sprang from my lights, its tail bouncing
waving like a handkerchief off in the dark.
Wherever I've lived I've driven at night: beach-
roads in Maine, waves burning white; one-lane
bridges, the ridges and hollows of West Virginia.
I've got a letter to mail, I'll say. And slip out.

Glide on back roads where I'll meet no other cars.
Roll by darkened houses, safe as graves, and think
I'm the only one in the whole county awake. Then
eyes ignite green in my lights. A white tail waves.
One night, in France, in the Alps, a wild boar,
a *sanglier,* stood in the road, all tusk and bristle.

I stopped. White peaks gathered behind him.
He stood there carved by my lights, a mad
and necessary thought, then ran from the road.
I watched him in a small silver field, turn,
run at the dogs, break through a thicket. Finally
I drove on with those white tusks flashing.

Sometimes, for fun, I'll let a radio preacher yell,
tell me how easy salvation is, how to "get saved."
It's as simple as the past tense. You only touch
the dial . . . mail in the tithe to Brother Sid.
Tonight what I need is that boar, the magic
of *sanglier*, a word full of blood; but even

as he breaks thickets in the mind, I see
the pork-butcher, *bon bourgeois,* string him up,
hang him from an ancient hook in front of his shop.
He turns slowly in the wind and into a small box
of sawdust under his snout drip the last drops
of that wild blood, gone, already absorbed.

To the Snow-walker

Space tells matter how to move;
matter tells space how to bend.
—"Einstein," PBS-TV

Enough!
That's probably what he said
to our white New England
street getting whiter
drifting high with snow—
cars useless.

Enough
of our tall front room
chilled with gray light
and the window where twigs bobbed
and pointed beyond themselves
for days.

Finally
he told all that white space
to get bent. On foot, into a scourge
of wind, he hiked toward the hospital
five miles away, Mom unvisited
for days.

Enough
of this foolishness, she said
before he joked about "All for Love"
but meant it. Then the last dark half
of his ten-mile orbit
the wind strong

enough
to blow him down near Mr. Donut.

But he made it back home, built a fire,
fell asleep at sixty-eight and
repeated that orbit for two more
snowy days.

Enough,
just enough pride in his voice
to move me long-distance
here in the sunbelt
where the only real snow is remembered.
And I wonder is it

enough
to know the white coming down
on what we do, covering all that matters,
making us enter the white space and
bend it with the small dark bodies
of our words.

Sixty-eight.
Ten miles. Us orbiting each other
in thought like small planets. Snow-walker
leaning into the white wind—
I can never think of this
enough.

Players

The yellow ball just clears the net, skids low.
Your racket reaches, flicks and floats it back.

We hit this poem together and watch it shuttle,
weave against the green of someone else's youth,

the emerald memory of a dozen different parks.
Back and forth, we build a rhythm, increase the pace,

then break. With lobs, then steady strokes again,
we stretch our rallies past the average-player five.

We make each other run, lunge to get what is past us,
play off the impossible. We do anything to outwit

the average, this space that is nothing without us.
Sometimes I take advantage, hit out hard, but you

still strain for the save, as if it were something rare,
important as marriage. So the ball leaves yellow lines.

Once, near the ocean, time did a radiant slo-mo.
You raced with your racket extended and the ball towered

to a yellow spot in a sky gone suddenly storm-green;
it hung while you centered in your white skirt; white,

yellow, storm-green, white—the perfect centering.
Too excited, I watched my overhead splash the net.

Then as now, we come together at the net, our faces glad
with sweat, each telling what the other missed, or didn't.

Acknowledgments

Grateful acknowledgment is made to editors of the following publications in which some of these poems or earlier versions of them first appeared:

Ecotone: "Laughing Gulls" and "Release";

The Georgia Review: "Running";

The Hudson Review: "A Lenten Observance," "Caught," "In The Daily Grind Café," "Trail";

The Louisville Review: "Awake" and "Gray Fox";

The News & Observer's Sunday Reader: "A Closing Season," "Getting There";

North American Review: "Spinners";

North Carolina Literary Review: "Deo Gratias";

Prairie Schooner: "Flounder Gigging," "Magdalene at the Mirror";

Rivendell: "Long Lens";

Tar River Poetry: "Stopping";

The Sewanee Review: "Back Again," "Out of Araviapa," "Ladybug," "Toledo, Spain";

"Cité Bleue," "Pilgrims," and "Last Run at La Plagne" were first collected and published with other poems as a chapbook entitled *Pilgrims* (Ampersand Press, 1987).

"Long Lens," "Getting There," and "Trail" were first collected and published with other poems as a chapbook entitled *Back Roads* (Independent Press, 2009).

"Long Lens" is for Sherryl Janosko

Special thanks to my wife Phyllis and my editor Thom Ward for reading the manuscript and providing me with invaluable suggestions for revision. Thanks as well to Debra Kang Dean and Philip Raisor for their critical reading of some early versions of various poems. I would also like to remember Leslie Norris, who died in 2006; a good friend and extraordinary writer, he was always very generous about reading my poems and stories, offering both criticism and encouragement over the years. Finally, I honor the memory of Al Poulin, founder of BOA Editions, teacher and my first editor.

About the Author

Peter Makuck taught at East Carolina University from 1976 to 2006. Founder of *Tar River Poetry* and its editor for almost thirty years, he was the English department's first Distinguished Professor. In 2008 he was Lee Smith Visiting Poet at North Carolina State University. His stories and poems, reviews and essays have appeared in *Poetry, The Nation, The Hudson Review, The Sewanee Review,* and *The Georgia Review.* In addition to four previous volumes of poems, four poetry chapbooks, and two collections of short stories, he has co-edited a book of essays, *An Open World,* on the Welsh poet Leslie Norris. His most recent collection of short stories *Costly Habits* (University of Missouri Press) was nominated for a PEN/Faulkner Award. Former Fulbright Exchange Professor to France, winner of the Brockman Award (given annually for the best collection of poetry by a North Carolinian), recipient of the Charity Randall Citation from the International Poetry Forum, juror for the annual Poet's Prize, he lives with his wife Phyllis on Bogue Banks, one of North Carolina's barrier islands.

BOA Editions, Ltd.
American Poets Continuum Series

Colophon

Long Lens: New & Selected Poems was set in Adobe Garamond Pro, a typeface created by Adobe type designer Robert Slimbach in 1989 based on the beauty and balance of the original Garamond typefaces. It's a digital interpretation of the roman types by Claude Garamond and the italic types of Robert Granjon.

The publication of this book is made possible, in part, by the special support of the following individuals:

Anonymous

Aaron & Lara Black

Gwen & Gary Conners

Mark & Karen Conners

Charles & Barbara Coté in memory of Charlie Coté Jr.

Susan DeWitt Davie

Peter & Suzanne Durant

Dane & Judy Gordon

Janice N. Harrington & Robert Dale Parker

Hugh Hennedy

Kip & Debby Hale

Michael Hall

Bob & Willy Hursh

Robin, Hollon & Casey Hursh in memory of Peter Hursh

X.J. & Dorothy M. Kennedy

Archie & Pat Kutz

Jack & Gail Langerak

Boo Poulin

Boo Poulin in memory of Debra Audet

Boo Poulin in honor of Susan Burke & Bill Leonardi

Steven O. Russell & Phyllis Rifkin-Russell

Peggy Savlov in memory of Peter Hursh

Vicki & Richard Schwartz

Rob Tortorella

Laura & Joe Wagner

Pat & Mike Wilder

Diana & Joe Zerella